The
Staffordshire
Village Book

THE VILLAGE BOOK SERIES

Other counties in this series include

The Staffordshire Village Book

Compiled by the Staffordshire
Federation of Women's Institutes from notes
sent by Institutes in the County

Published jointly by
Countryside Books, Newbury
and the SFWI, Stafford

First published 1988
© Staffordshire Federation of Women's Institutes 1988

Countryside Books
3 Catherine Road,
Newbury, Berkshire

Cover photograph is of Bramshall
by Freda Houldcroft

ISBN 1 85306 029 1

Produced through MRM Associates, Reading
Typeset by Acorn Bookwork, Salisbury
Printed in England by J.W. Arrowsmith, Bristol

Foreword

Welcome to Staffordshire, one of the largest Shire Counties situated in the centre of England.

It is a County of many changing scenes, from the Historic to the Industrial, but with a large proportion being rural, with productive farmlands set in beautiful countryside in which many delightful villages can be found and some of these villages are home to our Institutes.

The Federation is most grateful to W.I. Members and friends who have contributed articles for this book.

I hope when you have read The Staffordshire Village Book you will want to visit our County and I hope you will enjoy your visit as much as we have enjoyed compiling this book to commemorate our 70th Anniversary.

Margaret Kelly
County Chairman

Acknowledgements

The Staffordshire Federation of Women's Institutes would like to thank all those members and their Institutes who have worked so hard to research and provide information and drawings for their villages. Also a special thank you to Freda Houldcroft, co-ordinator for the project.

N

LEEK

Caldon Canal

STOKE-ON-TRENT

Trent & Mersey Canal

Shropshire Union Canal

STAFFORD

Staffs & Worcs. Canal

BURTON
UPON
TRENT

LICHFIELD

County of
STAFFORDSHIRE

Fifteenth century Church House at Abbots Bromley

Abbots Bromley 🖋️

The village of Abbots Bromley lies beautifully situated in the centre of the Needwood Forest plateau, about 115 metres above sea level and the name itself suggests a broom covered clearing in the woodland.

Abbots Bromley is famous for the Horn Dance, which takes place every year on the first Monday after 4th September. Six of the men taking part wear headpieces bearing ancient reindeer antlers. The Horns were carbon-dated in 1978 and results show them to date from 1065–80 and to be of domesticated castrated Reindeer, probably introduced by Northern invaders. The Horns are kept in the Hurst Chapel of the 14th century Abbots Bromley parish church, which is appropriately dedicated to St Nicholas.

For over 100 years the school of St Mary & St Anne has played an important part in the life of the village. St Anne's was opened in 1874 and St Mary's in 1882 the two being amalgamated in 1921. The school had a notable head-mistress in Marcia Alice Rice 1868–1958, a descendant of John Napier, the inventor of logarithms, and one of the first women to have BA and MA degrees conferred upon her.

One of the most noteworthy houses is that of Hall Hill Manor Farm where, in the year of 1586 Mary Queen of Scots reputedly rested on her way to Chartley from Tutbury, and again en route to her execution at Fotheringay. A pane of glass bearing an inscription to this effect was removed for safe-keeping and may be seen at the Salt Library in Stafford.

A reminder of the ancient forest can be recognised in the wood used in the half-timbered cottages and the lovely Church House which dates from around 1619. The even older Buttercross stands in the centre of the village with its grey slated roof supported on massive timber pillars.

Opposite the Buttercross is the Goats Head Inn which had, at one time, a room named after Dick Turpin where rumour declares that the highwayman stayed after stealing his famous horse, Black Bess, from Rugeley horse fair.

In the past there were at least 10 inns or ale houses in the village. Some of the names of these public houses were incorporated into a few lines of doggerel which used to be recited by a travelling showman who visited during the annual fair which was held at the feast of St Bartholomew, later known as Wakes week, and went as follows:

The *Ash Tree* shall no longer stand.
The Coach no more shall run.
We'll cast *the Dolphin* into the sea, only to be seen by
   the *Sailor Boy*.
We'll pull the horns off *the Goat* and cast away *the Crown*
We'll fell the *Royal Oak* and pull the *Blacks Head* down.
The Bagots shall hold their arms and *the Cock* shall crow no more.

The Coach, Goat, Crown, Royal Oak and the Bagot Arms still remain and together with five shops and a post office, local fire brigade, and an excellent modern health centre, the village is well served for all its needs.

Adbaston 🦢

The parish of Adbaston is still a quiet rural corner of Staffordshire, situated on the Staffordshire – Shropshire boundary, 12 miles west of Stafford. It is one of the largest and most sparsely populated parishes in the county, over 4,000 acres in extent and with a population of approximately 600. Its undulating free-draining farmland is described by a local farmer as 'honest land, which responds well to good management'. Besides Adbaston village the parish includes several scattered hamlets of which Bishops Offley and Knighton have the most houses.

The church of St Michael and All Angels is Adbaston's oldest and most interesting buiding. It is in the centre of the parish near where the old manor house stood. Dating from the 12th century some traces of its Norman construction can still be seen in the 2 lancet windows in the chancel. The tower was added in 1340, when the building was virtually complete. There are several ancient memorials inside the church and in the churchyard the foundations of the old preaching cross remain. It is older than the church.

In 1725 Adbaston Hall, a fine Georgian house, was built near the church to replace the old manor house. A property which pre-dates the Hall by a few years is the vicarage, now privately owned, and probably one of the oldest houses still in use in the village.

For over 300 years the villagers of Knighton have enjoyed a unique privilege. According to tradition villagers helped. Charles II to escape after the battle of Worcester in 1651. When the monarchy was restored in 1660 a special Act of Parliament was passed exempting the Knighton estate of 912 acres from all rates and taxes.

A milk-processing factory was built in 1911 by Cadbury Brothers next to the Shropshire Union Canal, which brought milk from the farms and linked the factory with the Bournville chocolate works. The factory is now owned by Premier Brands and it is still involved in food processing. In 1936 Cadbury Hall was built for the factory staff, but it has always been available for use by other organisations and is probably the main social centre for the parish.

Adbaston's school opened in 1843, the original building being part of today's enlarged First School, which has 24 pupils. The school is well-equipped and provides a balanced education for infants and juniors.

There is no village shop now, but Bishops Offley has a garage and a public house, The Brown Jug. Both The Jug and Knighton's Haber-dashers' Arms have horticultural clubs, and the latter holds a successful annual produce show. Both give generous support to local charities and the church.

Today farming is highly mechanised and does not employ large numbers, but many Adbaston people work at the local factory. The parish still has a miller. Six generations of the same family have worked the Offley Brook corn grinding water mill, which the miller believes is the only one in Staffordshire doing the work for which it was built. The mill is on the river Sow, part of the northern boundary of the parish.

In the same areas are two small nature reserves, Marsh Meadow and Offley Marsh Common. These reserves and the river banks contain interesting plants and attract abundant wildlife – birds, butterflies and small mammals. Wildfowl are frequently seen approaching and feeding on the pool at Offley Marsh and the mill pool at Offley Brook.

Alrewas

Alrewas, roughly translated means 'Alder Marsh' or a marshy area in a forest of mainly alder trees.

Alrewas has been in existence a long time but it is difficult to tell whether the Romans brought the road to Alrewas or whether more growth came to the area because of the roads – both Ryknild Street and Watling Street being very close.

The Trent and Mersey canal runs through the village providing good moorings with village shops for re-victualling, and also ample sport for the numerous anglers.

The building of the A38 dual carriageway and the bypass of the village by the road from Kings Bromley through to Tamworth has had the effect of enclosing the village and, dare one say it, drawing it back within itself. Take a brief glimpse back now to the first half of this century and begin at the western end of Main Street with The Navigation public house. Home Farm was there just before the bridge which was extremely steep in those days. Rebuilt in 1934 it bears the name of the Kent family, residents of the village for generations. Mr Arthur Kent, or 'Man Kent' as he was known, was a very skilled carpenter and also the verger.

Still on the same side of the road was the old bakehouse, baker's shop and, of course, the inevitable smallholding. On the opposite bank of the canal from Home Farm was the wheelwright, whose thatched cottage still stands. Across the road the village shop is still there today, as are also what used to be the estate workers' houses of the Earl of Lichfield who, at the time, owned most of the land.

Of the several farms – at least six – the farmhouses were in Main Street but most of the land was outside the village, stretching out to Kings Bromley, Croxall, Wychnor, along the main road and the canal. The railway station, which stood where the crossings are now, was in those days used by most of the village in some way. Farmers brought milk to be despatched around the area, a good percentage of villagers went to work in the breweries in Burton and those of the children who aspired to grammar school also made use of the very busy station.

Then there were the osier beds between the river and the canal where the special willow was grown for the basketmaker to ply his essential skills. Of course, there was the full quota of hostelries, not necessarily all the same ones standing today although several have been serving the village throughout the century. Finish at the eastern end of Main Street with the Paul Pry, which was the old coaching station.

Alsagers Bank 🍃

Situated on a southern spur of the Pennine Chain, the village enjoys a view unrivalled for miles. To the west the fertile plains of Cheshire, bisected by the M6; beyond, the dramatic backcloth of the Long Mynd, the Wrekin and Berwyn Mountains, often with snow-capped peaks glistening in the morning sun; to the north Jodrell Bank telescope and beyond, the tower of Liverpool's Anglican Cathedral. The stark Buxton hills stand to the east and as dusk falls the million lights of the Potteries illuminate the night sky.

Why Alsagers Bank? Legend has it that Mr Alsager lived at the bottom of the hill – too steep for one horse, so he loaned extra horses to travellers to pull their heavy loads to the top, hence Alsagers Bank (Owgis Bonk to the locals).

The 18th century brought the discovery of coal, and the collier, in his delf rags (pit clothes) carrying his snappin' tin and water bottle, his metal tipped wooden soled clogs clanging along the cobbled street on his way to the pit. Synonymous with coal were the Heathcoates, squires of Apedale Hall, and local mine owners. Apedale Hall was demolished in 1934.

The Heathcote family were local benefactors. Heathcote County Primary School, was their gift to the village. Two cottages opposite the school gates were originally an orphanage, also donated by the family. Built in 1839, the school has turned out some notable scholars.

St John's church was also donated by the family, some of whom are buried in the churchyard on the hill. In the shelter on the same hillside stands the simple memorial to the fallen of the two World Wars.

The area grew rich on 'black diamonds', but at a price. There is no more poignant chapter in the history of mining than Saturday, 12th January 1918, the bleak snowy day when an explosion at the Minnie Pit claimed the lives of 155 men and boys – 44 of them 16 and under, 22 only 14 and one boy of 13 who was looking forward to collecting his first week's wages that day.

The 1930s brought change. Mines closed, land reverted to nature and became a habitat for wildlife, a place where children played and lovers did their courting to the accompaniment of songbirds' chorus and the perfume of wild flowers. The square chimney of Watermills Colliery still stands in the Apedale Valley and three tablets, much eroded by time and the elements, on the sides of the chimney exhort us to 'Be Just and Fear Not', 'Live and Let Live' and 'Regard the End'. Despite vociferous protests from conservationists, British Coal are now opencasting the area.

Inseparable from the mines were the Methodist chapels now, unfortunately demolished. Old people's bungalows occupy the site of one of these, a far cry from the old cottages, known locally as 'Stir Pudding Row' which once stood adjacent to the chapel. The spirit of Methodism still lives in the hearts of older villagers.

The mines have closed, there is no industry and the village is a dormitory for commuters, many be car, to Newcastle and the Potteries and north to Cheshire. The village still has a post office, newsagent and general store.

Alton ༄

Alton stands on the steep southern side of the Churnet Valley, on the north side of which is the well know leisure park of Alton Towers.

Formerly known as 'Alverton', the village dates from Saxon times and is described in Domesday as having two ploughs and waste.

The ruins of a Norman castle overhang the valley along with the 19th century castle and Roman Catholic church built by John the 16th Earl of Shrewsbury. Nearby is the 11th century parish church of St Peter. In addition to the two churches, there have been, in the past, four Non-Conformist chapels, only one of which is now in use.

This mixture of various denominations has made the village somewhat unusual, for long before the present ecumenical movement, Anglicans, Catholics and Methodists lived happily together, inter-marrying and forming one community.

Before the Second World War, the majority of people worked at the copper works of Thomas Bolton at Oakamoor and Froghall and travelled each day by train, as hardly anyone had a car. At tea time each day groups of children would go to the station to meet Dad off the train and carry home his snapping basket. The railway line was axed by Dr Beeching in the 1960s.

November was quite a lucrative month for village children. On All

Souls Day, 2nd November, they went knocking on doors and 'Soul-caking'. The words they sang went something like this:

Soul-cake, a soul cake, pretty good day for a soul cake,
Woo-oo, an apple or two, if you have no apples, pears will do.
Pray good mistress get out your keys, go down to the cellar, get what
you please
Apple, pear, plum or cherry, or anything else to make us all merry.
The roads are very dirty, my shoes are very thin, but I've got a
pocket to put a penny in
If you haven't got a penny, a half penny will do, if you haven't got a
half penny, God Bless you.

This and other ditties have not been heard for the last 50 years. The modern equivalent of 'Trick or treat' has taken their place.

The 29th May is often referred to as 'Oak Apple Day'. In this village it was called 'Oak and Nettle Day'. On the way to school, the boys would gather bunches of nettles with which to sting the legs of anyone not wearing a sprig of oak leaves. This custom commemorates the return of King Charles II from exile on 29th May 1660, and the restoration of the monarchy.

In the early 1970s the village went through quite a revolution when new estates were built. Happily many of the newcomers have put down their roots and are now taking an important part in village life.

Amington 🐿️

Life in the village of Amington has been recorded since Saxon times. The earlier buildings were 'travellers' rests' for monks journeying between the various manasteries and other religious houses which formed a network under the patronage of St Editha. The Repington family purchased the land and buildings after the Dissolution of the Monasteries.

The present church is a beautiful building with a lovely reredos, a gift of a Repington of the time. St Editha is depicted carrying the church in her arms on the processional staff kept near the choir stalls.

The Methodist church has been in Amington for a considerable time and the present building is nearly 100 years old. It is warm and comfortable and there is a tradition of friendliness and good singing. One of the most notable men was Mr Roland Davis who died in 1967. He was a boat-builder with a love of music and attached to the Amington Silver Prize Band of which his father was, at that time, the conductor. As his love of music grew he studied and went to university where his fellow students were Barbirolli and Malcolm Sargent. There is a plaque to his memory in the church.

The Church of England school was over 100 years old when it closed and had served the village well. New schools, Greenacre and Florendine Primary and Woodhouse Senior Modern School replaced the old one.

Amington has always had plenty of family businesses such as butchers (with slaughterhouses) grocers and greengrocers, fish and chip shops, barbers etc. and the same is true today.

Tamworth Road is, as the name suggests, the way into (and out of) Tamworth and is the main road to outlying villages such as Newton Regis and Austrey (in North Warwickshire). The village was, itself, in North Warwickshire until about 1965 when it was absorbed into Tamworth Borough and consequently into Staffordshire.

In the days of coal and steam Amington had its own mine and there were several in the immediate vicinity. Agriculture was another industry where men were employed and the women worked in tailoring or tape making. On the Amington Industrial Estate small engineering works and many other modern businesses have started since the mine closed.

If Tamworth Road is one boundary in Amington then Woodland Way, Kerria Road and Sandy Lane provide another, for up there are the thousands of homes designed and built for Birmingham Corporation to house their overspill.

The river, railway and canal run practically parallel through Amington. The river and canal provide pleasure to anglers and visitors and most pubs are near enough to provide meals and entertainment. People who cannot recall the name of the village still remember happy times spent at The Pretty Pigs inn. The railway station is on two levels and provides transport to Scotland or London, Cornwall or Kilmarnock. The canal also carries a lot of pleasure cruisers and narrow boats during the season and freight all the year round. Due to mining subsidence the river swells into some very large pools at the Warwickshire end of the village, which are patrolled as a nature reserve. Although most of Amington is now built up there is quite a lot of green and pleasant land to be found around the pools and across the meadows.

16

Anslow 🐚

The village of Anslow, formed in 1861, was originally a hamlet on the edge of Needwood Forest and is situated on the eastern boundary of the parish close to the outskirts of Burton upon Trent. The name Anslow is derived from names meaning pastureland, including Ansedeley and Ansley.

The church, formerly called Needwood church was built in Norman style in 1850 by the Mosley family, great landowners who lived at nearby Needwood. Prior to the church being built, the parishioners gathered at a well in the centre of the village to be taken into Rolleston for their services. Unfortunately, the well has now disappeared, as have the numerous ponds which have been filled in and drained. A Methodist chapel was built before the church in 1828.

The old school is now a private dwelling house next to the church and a new one was built in 1909, also by the Mosley family.

Agriculture is the main occupation in the village, which has neither post office or shop, only quite recently a farm shop. The village blacksmith who stood 'opposite the spreading chestnut tree' has now passed on, but the forge, on another site, now manufactures wrought iron items, including gates, signs etc. Although there is a small development of private dwellings, the residents have their own occupations which take them away from the village.

The Bell Inn no doubt was named after the bell which was rung on the site of the building in times of danger and to guide those lost in the forest. Apparently, bell ringing was also a deterrent to goblins, witches and warlocks. The inn at the southern end of the parish was so called after the gate to the Brend Wood or Burnt Wood and so eventually became the Burnt Gate.

The village hall was built in 1952, funded by a grant and various efforts by the parishioners themselves. Although it is used regularly the standard of upkeep and general appearance was rewarded in 1967 by winning an award for the Best Kept Hall. Five years earlier in 1962, Anslow won the Best Kept Village award.

In the centre of the village stands the original wooden three-finger signpost. This will be replaced by another wooden one in preference to the modern ones used elsewhere.

The thatched cottage, part of it dating back to the 16th century, was

17

the only dwelling shown on very old maps. Having been rethatched it is now guarded over by an owl as a deterrent to the birds who favour thatch as a roosting place.

There are families still living in the parish whose ancestors go back as far as the 16th century and at one time most of the inhabitants were inter-related.

The village of Anslow

Armitage-with-Handsacre 🌿

About AD 1100 a hermit came to live among the rocks upon which the church of St John the Baptist now stands. This 'hermitage' eventually gave the village of Armitage its name.

Originally Handsacre was the more important, being mentioned in the Domesday Book. The arable land of about 500 acres was held by the Lords of the Manor of Hadesacre.

As one approaches the village from Rugeley, Hawkesyard Priory can be seen. Hawkesyard, once the seat of the de Ruggeleyes, fell into a ruinous state. The original ancient site is now covered by the stretch of water owned by the power station. The present house was built in 1760 and was first called Armitage Park. It was occupied in 1839 by Mary Spode and her son Josiah IV, who reverted to the original name of the house – Hawkesyard. Josiah married in 1848 and was at this time a practising Anglican. A few years after the rebuilding of Armitage church a vestry and organ chapel were added by Josiah and later he purchased a new organ for Lichfield Cathedral and had the old one installed in Armitage church, where he was appointed organist in 1866. Built 1789–91 by Samuel Green, this organ is the last, largest and best preserved of the classical style of English Organ building. It is in fact the only completely restored 18th century cathedral size organ left and is still in use.

Josiah later converted to the Catholic faith and the property was given to the Dominican Order. A small group arrived in 1894 and two years later levelling of the site for the priory began. This building programme continued until 1914 when war was declared and more recently the priory and Spode House were used as a Conference Centre.

In 1986 the remains of Handsacre Hall and its moat were examined by archaeologists. The moat dates from the 12th century and the Hall was originally built in the 14th century. Unfortunately little remains, but the site of the Hall has been designated as of historical interest and it is required to be protected when the land around is developed.

Due to the presence of clay in the area a number of small brickworks sprang up in both Armitage and Handsacre. Clay from Stile Cop was made into clay pipes at Pipe Place Farm, which is on the road out of Handsacre to Abbots Bromley. Eventually these small industries disappeared, but a pottery was started in 1817 by Thomas Bond. The business passed through several changes of ownership and had closed down by 1850. In 1851 it was taken over by Salt and Swan who began the manufacture of sanitary ware for the first time. By 1867 the Rev Edward Johns had bought the business and his son later sold out to ER and AH Corn in 1900. The name of the company changed from Edward Johns and Co Ltd to Armitage Ware, and then joined with Shanks to form Armitage Shanks Group Ltd. In 1980 Blue Circle Cement made a successful bid for the company.

With the building of Lea Hall Colliery at Rugeley, a housing estate was built at Handsacre to provide accommodation for the miners, who came from the North of England to work there. Most of the jobs in the area are therefore in the pottery and mining industries.

Ashley 🐦

The picturesque village of Ashley is in the quiet north-west corner of the county separated from the busy Newcastle-Market Drayton road by a network of high-hedged, quiet country lanes. The small village remains much the same as it was 100 years ago. Time and the motor car have brought some change, but the brunt of this has been borne by nearby Loggerheads with its modern shops, housing estates and mainly commuter population.

For over 700 years the parish church has watched over the village and is a record of its history. Legend states it was built by a knight, David Kenric, in gratitude for being led safely out of the surrounding forests when on his way to join the Black Prince in France for the battle of Crecy (1346). Today, a magnificent alabaster tomb, the largest in a parish church in England, built in 1603 by Thomas, Lord Gerard, stands side-by-side with Victorian monuments to the Kinnersley and Meynell Ingram families. Over the chancel arch the black basalt funerary urn was made by Josiah Wedgwood himself in memory of his friend and benefactor, Sir William Chetwynd of Ingestre. In the early 18th century the last of the Gerard family staked his Ashley estates in a game of cards. He lost to Littleton Poinz Meynell and this gave Ashley a new Lord of the Manor and a new legend.

Recorded in the Domesday Survey as Esselie, Ashley lay in the heart of the forest and heathland that covered north-west Staffordshire. Meaning 'a clearing in the ashwoods' the tiny hamlet had to provide 'four men and a net' for the Bishop of Lichfield whenever he chose to hunt in the Bishop's Wood. Little of the great forest remains today. Most has been turned into pasture. Bishop's Wood and Burnt Wood lie on the western border. The charcoal burners of Burnt Wood provided the refugee Huguenots with fuel for their furnaces in Bishop's Wood. There they manufactured glass in the time of Queen Elizabeth I. Now Forestry Commission property, the woods provide glorious walks for the local people.

Before the beginning of the 19th century, life carried on in Ashley as it had for generations. Men worked on the land or as foresters or blacksmiths. Women helped on the farms or were in domestic service. At Hookgate wooden crates were made to transport the pottery made in the nearby Potteries. Thanks to the generosity of the Kinnersley and Meynell families there was a National School in Ashley in 1822. The sound of the bell called the children to school. In 1960 children still queued up for the honour of ringing the same bell. In 1970, because of the rising numbers, the children were transferred to the present modern building at Loggerheads. It is said that the heart went out of the village.

The old school is now the Health Centre and village library. Many of the old cottages and houses still lie close by.

In the early 1900s Ashley became a place of weekend pilgrimage for the people of the Potteries. They came by pony and trap, later by charabanc to the Meynell Arms or the Loggerheads Hotel for ham and egg teas.

On nearby Ashley Heath, tucked away among the pines and birches are modern houses. Many began their lives as railway carriages, weekend homes for the townsfolk. Some were retreats for those suffering from the dreaded chest diseases contracted in the pot-banks or mines. They came for the pure clean air of the pinewoods. Later the sanatorium was built at Loggerheads to treat these diseases. Now thanks to modern medicine the sanatorium is no more – in its place a pleasant estate of modern houses.

Aston-by-Stone ✤

Most people are attracted to Aston by the pretty silhouette of the spire of St Saviour's and the old church school nestling amongst the trees. The parish church was built in the Early English style during the 1840s by local landowners, the Parker-Jervis family.

Unusually for such a small village there is another church – the Catholic church of St Michael in the grounds of Aston Hall. This house was bequeathed for the use of a Roman Catholic community, and the Hall is now run by a small group of nuns who care for sick and aging clergy. The relics of St Chad were rediscovered in the chapel at Aston Hall in 1838, where they had been hidden during the Reformation. They now lie in St Chad's cathedral in Birmingham. Further evidence that Aston has long been a Catholic stronghold is that Cardinal Newman is reputed to have been converted to Catholicism whilst staying here in around 1843. The present Hall was rebuilt in 1855 on the site of the original moated mansion. Legend has it that a cross on the Hall's boundary wall marks the spot where a monk was killed by lightning.

Another mansion of note is Pirehill House, now the home of the Staffordshire Fire Brigade Headquarters. The house is not visible from the road, but their aerial can be seen sprouting from the encircling trees. Nearby is a large pond used for private fishing. On its banks is an old osier bed, reflecting the proximity of the Potteries, which required a plentiful supply of baskets for transporting their products. A stream runs down to the pool at Aston Farm, right by the main road. At one time this provided the power for a waterwheel. This wheel, which still exists, was used not only to grind corn, but earlier this century to power a milking machine.

The name Aston is probably derived from the Anglo-Saxon for 'Ashtown'. It is an ancient crossing point – a ford or bridge has existed since the 15th century, and pre-dates the bridge in Stone. The main road from Stafford to Stone crossed the Trent in Aston until the Stafford-Stone turnpike was opened in 1761. The former is now a quiet lane, but it can be another scene of unexpected encounters – the canal bridge is narrow, hump-backed and on a bend – take care! Between these two bridges is a raised walk-way as this area is prone to flooding.

A walk along the canal towpath can be most rewarding. It is entertaining to watch the narrow boats negotiating the lock, and the banks are rich in wild flowers such as tansy and meadow cranesbill. There is an old wharf at Mill Farm, the site of a water-powered flint mill. Ground flints were also required by the Potteries.

In Aston Lane is the village oak, planted in 1911 to commemorate the coronation of King George V. This stands near a striking Tudor house, Yew Tree Cottage, whose timbers are probably over 500 years old, and used for a different structure originally. Further down the lane is a pretty thatched cottage, Willow Farm.

Old routes which have never been metalled make pleasant footpaths. One old route cuts across the fields to the Three Crowns at Little Stoke. This community is part of the parish of Aston-by-Stone, and the site of Aston's railway station until its closure in 1964. Nearby is Brassworks Farm, where evidence of the old Works is often unearthed.

The diversity and number of trades in Aston has dwindled during this century, and there has been little recent development. However, it is a thriving farming community with an active social life centred on the village hall and The Crown.

Audley 🎋

Audley, an out of the way quiet place, stands on the top of a hill overlooking the Cheshire plain, at the extreme north-west of Stafford-shire. Domesday reference calls it 'Aldidelege' after the female owner of the land. Bordering the main route to Chester, it was used as a stop-off point by Roman foot soldiers; standing on a hill, the Normans used it as a vantage point and built a stronghold, the motte still faintly discernible; Offa's Dyke protected it from early ravages of war.

Seventeenth century financial troubles led to the land being split in smaller units, owned by familiar names still in existence, Eardley, Row-ley, Vernon etc. Edward Vernon founded Audley's first grammar school in 1611. It finally closed in 1900 but an endowment still exists to assist scholarship children.

Land owners in the 17th and 18th centuries made many charitable provisions for the poor and in 1734 a workhouse was built. Prosperity increased with the advent of the small ironworks and nail making, followed by an increase in the scale of coal mining, but in 1840 a census revealed an above average illiteracy in the village. In 1900 a new school was opened and by the 1950s Audley was known as 'the village of teachers', so many people having entered the profession.

The church of St James, built on an existing 13th century site, and the oldest part being 14th century, gave Audley its spiritual and cultural background. Benefactors throughout the ages have helped to maintain the fabric. It has a fine 14th century brass rubbing of Thomas de Audley and just visible in the wall is a lepers' peep hole. In the church's old records is recorded a 'great sweat' as killing 29 people in 1551.

In 1884 Charles Phillip Wilbraham was appointed vicar – a much travelled and scholarly man. A major benefactor of the church, he turned down a Bishopric to stay in Audley. When disaster struck a pit at Talke killing 91 men, he traversed the countryside raising funds for the dependants. The old vicarage named after him is now Wilbraham House old peoples' home.

Methodism finally came officially to Audley with a meeting held in Hullockspool Farm at the beginning of the 19th century. In 1896, the Primitive Methodists built a fine chapel to house a congregation of 600 and spiritually split the village. But, with Methodism came music. Elijah Wareham wrote beautiful anthems (still being sung today). Bob Herod founded the Audley Prize band and formed the first male voice choir. It took William Bowers to blend the church and chapel choristers in annual renditions of the *Messiah*, and for over 25 years he led the Audley male voice choir in competition singing.

The closure of ironworks and the rundown of coal mining led to a decline in population. However, the structure of the village has changed very little, as recorded by local 19th century photographer Thomas Wareham. His wonderful range of photographs of people and their social activities has been published by his daughter for posterity.

Some buildings have disappeared, for instance the Primitive chapel site is now taken up by a supermarket and new additions include a Health Centre, library, Pensioners' Hall, banks, and a variety of shops. The old cinema now houses the very successful Audley Players – as can be seen the village is completely self sufficient.

Amongst the celebrities of the village is 'Jabez', otherwise known as Wilf Bloor, an expert on the North Staffordshire dialect, having written over 250 short stories published in 3 books. He describes himself as 'a country lad wot larkes tellin teeles abite t' owd dees'.

24

Bagnall

The picturesque village of Bagnall is situated about 6 miles outside the Potteries. The name Bagnall is derived from the Anglo-Saxon name Bagga. It is not mentioned in the Domesday Book, this area being described as wasteland.

The ancient cross still standing on the village green is surrounded by trees planted by the parish councillors in 1905, and although there are no records that a market was held here it is thought that in medieval times when the plague was raging round the country, the local farmers brought their produce to the cross where the townspeople were able to collect it under supervision, to make sure they did not come into contact with each other.

Behind the cross stands Bagnall Hall, rebuilt several times and bearing the dates 1603 and 1777. Part of the old house of 1603 is still standing but has been enlarged. The fine doorway opens onto a handsome Jacobean staircase. The windows are in recess with strong panels and the ceiling is ornamented by beams crossing each other. It was the residence of William Murhall who died in 1762 and was buried in Endon churchyard. One of the many legends surrounding Bagnall village says that William Murhall, at the time of the 1745 Jacobite Rebellion, had one of the Pretender's soldiers flayed alive, in revenge for the mutilation he had undergone by some of the troops (hence the name of the nearby hamlet of Tom(s)kin).

On the left of the old market cross is the church built about 1834 and enlarged in 1880 with the addition of a chancel. This church replaced a much smaller structure on the same site. It was a very small building which might easily have been taken for a barn had it not been for the wooden belfry that contained one small solitary curfew bell which was rung at sunset in summer and 8 pm in winter.

The east window of the new church is of French glass purchased at Amiens, and was placed in the church in 1883 by the Rev S H Owen who is buried in the churchyard. The pictures on the walls were painted by John Thorley, a local artist in 1881. There is also a memorial to Mr Yates by whose bequest loaves were distributed to the poor every Christmas. The pulpit is a fitting memorial to those who fell in the First and Second World Wars.

The annual Cake Fair in aid of church funds was one of the traditional events of the year held one day during Whit week which attracted many visitors from all over the surrounding district. A well-known public figure was usually asked to perform the opening ceremony. One of the first Cake Fairs was held in the large room of the village inn. Why it was called a Cake Fair nobody really knows but there was always a good supply of cakes!

This area of isolated farmsteads and few cottages has changed in recent years. The school never reopened after it burned down in the 1960s. The mill, so active in the 18th century was never repaired and the stone was used for other buildings. Farming continues, machines replacing men and horses, but most of the inhabitants travel to work in the nearby towns. But look beyond the new building, to the hills, the hedgerows and the old stone buildings, and there are many reminders of what the village of Bagnall once was.

Baldwin's Gate 🐚

Looking at the village of Baldwin's Gate today with its modern housing estates one cannot imagine what it was like at the beginning of the 19th century. Its name derived from a Mr Baldwin, who was the toll-gate keeper.

The railway station was a very busy place, built around 1850, believed to be one of the first in the Potteries on land sold by the local squire – Mr Cavenagh-Mainwaring of Whitmore. This was used to despatch pottery ware all over the country, trains running five times daily between Crewe and Stafford.

The Sheet Anchor public house was built in 1853 by Admiral Mainwaring, hence the name. Every alternate Monday a cattle auction was held in a building a few yards away from The Sheet Anchor and cattle were driven in from a wide area, afterwards being loaded on to trains and transported to slaughter-houses in Stafford and Crewe.

On the opposite side of the road was a second toll-house and here the doctors held their surgeries. This was demolished in the 1960s and a chalet house built, still bearing the name 'Toll-Gate House'.

Further on stands a chapel and three cottages built in 1859 and still in use today, adjoining a grocery shop and post office, a bakery being added in 1927.

At the end of the village were three sand holes, a lot of places in the village bearing the word 'sand' today eg Sandy Lane and Sandyfields. The sand from these was transported daily to the station and onwards to Crewe, to be used for mouldings in the railway trade.

Beyond is Slymans Dale and this was the scene of cock fighting, attended by miners from Madeley and the Potteries.

At the cross roads the road leads to Madeley, which was then the estate of Lord Crewe, whose name and coat of arms can be seen on various buildings and a farmhouse in the village. Baldwin's Gate was once part of the Madeley estate.

Barlaston

Barlaston lies to the north of the county, between Stone and Newcastle, just off the busy A34, which was the main London to Chester road in times past. In the Domesday Book of 1086 it is referred to as Bernulvestone.

Today Barlaston is known all over the world as the home of Wedgwood pottery, with many overseas visitors coming for business and pleasure. The current Wedgwood factory was built here between 1938 and 1940 on the Barlaston Hall estate. This estate was purchased from the Broughton-Adderley family in 1936. The final move from Etruria was not completed until 1950, because of the intervention of the Second World War. A model village was built near the factory for key workers, and the whole was set within the beautifully landscaped park of Barlaston Hall, which was laid out in the 18th century.

Barlaston Hall has been featured in the national press, because of its architectural merit and its sad state of repair. Happily, it is now owned by the Save England's Heritage Society, who are renovating it. The Hall stands high on a wooded ridge and can be clearly seen from miles around. It was built in 1756 by Thomas Mills, an attorney from Leek. It featured on the dinner service made by Wedgwood for the Empress Catherine of Russia in 1773 and, latterly, during the Second World War was the headquarters of the Bank of England.

Barlaston Hall, whose estate houses the world famous Wedgwood pottery factory

The former village school is a picturesque white-washed building standing on the village green, by the war memorial. It dates from the end of the 18th century, when it replaced earlier Dame schools. It was established and endowed by Thomas Mills of Barlaston Hall, and flourished until 1963, when it was replaced by a large modern building. It now houses a branch of the County Library.

Until the end of the 18th century Barlaston was isolated, and its inhabitants worked on the land. This gradually changed with the building of the Trent and Mersey canal and the railway. The advent of the canal gave rise to boat building, and this continued until the 1920s. The workers' cottages still stand by the canal. The establishment of the railway led to the well-to-do from Stoke moving out of town to live in Barlaston, and commuting to work.

There has been a place of worship in Barlaston since the early 13th century. The former church, dating partly from the early 16th century, and dedicated to St John the Baptist, was declared unsafe and has been replaced by a new one near the village green. This was consecrated in 1984. In the 19th century parish wakes were held to celebrate the feast of St John's nativity, but alas these gradually died out. In the 1930s, the church fete, held on the village green, was instigated to, in some way, carry on this tradition. It is an event much enjoyed by the villagers to this day.

Older residents can remember when the village was self-sufficient, with its own slaughter-house, tanyard, shoe-maker, blacksmith, bakery and local shop, and even now there is a good range of shops, a hairdresser, garage, two public houses and an excellent Health Centre, reflecting the growth in population. However, it is still a village at heart, with a strong sense of identity and a flourishing community life.

Barton under Needwood 🦌

The Saxon settlement at Catholme on the Trent gravel terrace (excavated in 1976) later migrated northwards, unscathed by the Danes, to develop as Barton, 1¼ miles away. The Domesday Book records that the king held Barton's 360 acres.

Life has changed today, with the population in 1985 over 4,920, five new estates and much in-filling among the older buildings on Main Street and elsewhere. These shops and cottages, clad in 19th century entrepreneur Sam Coulson's bricks, conceal their beamed Tudor origins. Nikolaus Pevsner, the architectural historian, commented on the large village houses, and particularly the church which 'will not easily be forgotten'. There was a church here in 1157, which vanished without trace. The present church, begun in 1517, owes its origin to Henry VII who came here to hunt and met William Taylor, a forest game warden and father of triplet boys. They were shown to the king who saw in them a sign of the Holy Trinity, and promised to educate them if they grew to manhood. All three survived and became Doctors of Canon Law. John, the eldest, rose highest to be King's Clerk to Henry VIII, Clerk to Parliament and Master of the Rolls.

John inherited his father's cottage and lands, and there endowed his new church, which, apart from Victorian widening, retains its Tudor proportions. The unusual chancel, a three-sided apse, contains Taylor's windows, much restored, showing his coat-of-arms. The ancient parish chest and pre-Reformation chalice are all that remain from the earlier church. Religious fashion later changed its name from St Mary Magdalen to St James. It contains the modern war memorial Chapel of Peace.

Barton has a long history of caring for the poor. Since the 1601 Poor Law Act, money was levied for overseers to carry out this duty and early in the 1700s a workhouse was built. Charity boards in the church tell their own story of countless bequests. One merits special mention. In 1651 William Key of Sherholt Lodge willed land in Barton for the poor and 10 shillings to the priest for a sermon on Good Friday. Today's trustees see both continue. Several charities were combined to benefit the needy. Not all amenities are in the past, the 100 year old Cottage Hospital still nurses the sick and next door the new Health Centre cares for the community. Also in Short Lane is the Fire Station manned by retained firemen.

The Central Hall, one-time meeting place for many events, was demolished by compulsory order in 1985, uniting the village in a co-ordinated effort to build a new village hall in Crowberry Lane. The church hall built in 1977, caters for many organisations.

Six public houses welcome customers and willingly foster charities. The Domesday Plaque has been fixed outside The Shoulder of Mutton.

Education came early with a Free School founded in 1593 by Thomas Russell of the Drapers' Company. It has passed into history, but his name is retained by the Infant and Junior Schools. The High School bears John Taylor's name.

Where the barley which gave Barton its name 'Barley-ton' (Barley-homestead) once flourished, new homes continue to grow.

Betley 🌿

The village of Betley, situated on the thoroughfare between the ancient towns of Newcastle and Nantwich, was recorded in the Domesday Book of 1086.

By 2nd May 1227 Betley had been granted a charter whereby a market might be held each Thursday, after which the village carried the title of Borough. The population in 1298 is thought to have been 360. As a borough Betley depended on some 20 neighbouring villages to sustain its market. Betley's inhabitants developed as craftsmen, small business men and traders alongside its agricultural and horticultural workers.

Betley Court was built in 1716 and in the 1790s was owned by Sir Thomas Fletcher. In this horticultural area it is not surprising to find the encouragement of gardening. Betley Court had its formal gardens, walled kitchen garden (which has become the site of six executive-type houses known as Court Walk), lawns, dingle and ice-house. The 'big house' employed a head gardener (who lived in what is still known as Gardener's Cottage) and other gardeners, while the cottagers were encouraged to grow good produce in their own gardens. Hence the establishment of Betley Show well over 100 years ago.

Adjoining Betley Court is 'the home farm', built in 1885 and now known as Betley Court Farm. One of its large fields became the obvious site for the Betley Show each year. This traditional show has continued annually until the present day. To suit modern requirements the show changed from the first Wednesday to the first Saturday in August during the 1960s.

The latest project undertaken in Betley is the formation of the Sportsground Committee whose commission is to develop the piece of land adjoining the village hall to provide future leisure activities for the village. Photographs show that both Betley and neighbouring Wrinehill have boasted notable cricket and football teams since at least 1880. Now there are plans for tennis courts and a bowling green.

In more recent years the idea of holding a market in the main road of Betley has been revived. In 1961 and 1964 Midsummer Markets were held to raise funds to build the village hall, while in 1977 was celebrated the 700th anniversary of the granting of the charter and in 1985 a further Midsummer Market was held to raise funds towards the roof of the 12th century church.

Biddulph Moor 🌿

Early in the 19th century Biddulph Moor was three parishes – Horton, Greenway Moor and Bradley Green, becoming Greenway Moor and finally Biddulph Moor. Trent Well is here – the start of the river Trent. The village was made up of a church, church school (until 1909 when the council school was built), Primitive chapel and Wesleyan chapel and two public houses. Unusual for a village, each place of worship has its own burial ground, still in use today. Parlour windows were used as a shop by one or two enterprising women.

Small-holdings were dotted around the outskirts and the men mostly went to work in the pits, 'delf', or stoneholes, hewing the coal and stone. Stone built houses still stand as a reminder of the craftsmen of those days. Wives stayed at home, rearing large families. One lady had 24 pregnancies, with 21 babies living and for her efforts she received a letter from the Queen! Almost everyone wore clogs on the moor; tips were always coming off, so a clogger's shop did a good trade.

Greenway Moor had a very good Prize Band, which was very competitive, winning prizes as far afield as London. This brass band is still very active and is now known as the Greenway Moor Selectus Band.

Legend has it that the folk of the Moor were descended from the Saracens, brought back from the Crusades by the Biddulf family of Biddulph Old Hall, to be their servants. The Moor is noted for its dialect, still spoken by some of the inhabitants today which differs considerably from the 'Potteries' dialect.

Nicknames were very much in evidence on the Moor. There were so many families of the same name – the Baileys, Browns, Nixons and

Stanways, so there were the 'Pinkies', 'Blues', Blackens', 'Ducks' and others too numerous to mention.

Biddulph Moor lies at the end of the Pennine Range, running from Troughstones, to Bailey's Hill and Wickenstone Rocks. Views from the top of Troughstones are fantastic and on a clear day one can see the Welsh hills and even as far as Liverpool. Well worth the climb.

In 1897 a borehole was sunk at Nettlebeds Farm, water was then pumped to a reservoir on the west side of the Moor. Others had to carry water in buckets with a yoke on their shoulders from Trent Well or the Gruel Spout. The latter has never been known to run dry, even during the drought of 1976. When there is a restriction on the use of water, you will see people taking their cars to the Spout to wash them. The water is pure and sparkling and it is a fact that men collect the water to drink with their whisky – far better than water from the tap.

As the community grew with more houses and bungalows, the need for a village hall was talked about and so fund raising started, with well dressing at the Trent Well, parades, and so on. Now the hall is built and is always fully booked for weddings, dances, playgroups, fayres, etc.

Bignall End 🐌

Bignall End, in the parish of Audley, can trace its history back more than 1,000 years. Today the area covered by Bignall End is within the borough of Newcastle-under-Lyme.

There is no longer any village industry as such here now, but on agricultural land and reclaimed colliery land there are three housing estates, which almost link up to Audley, the next village. Bignall End has vastly changed over the past few years from a small village in the country, with a closely-knit community where everyone knew each other.

In the 18th century it was usual for each house to have a piece of land to cultivate, as there were mostly many small houses scattered about the countryside, but as the land at Bignall End was very rich in coal (which enabled the land owners of the area to become very rich and prosperous) many of the men would be working as ground colliers besides being tanners and thatchers.

Another industry which grew and flourished in the 18th century was nail making and families would work in their own homes or outbuildings making nails for use in building. Many of these families lived on Boon Hill, and today one of these cottages still remains, although extended and modernised.

Bignall End is very proud of its Cricket Club. Cricket began here in the 1870s, originally at Tibb's Craft until 1884 when it found a better site at Bignall End Hall.

One of the most tragic events of Bignall End worthy of special mention is the disaster at the Diglake Colliery on 14th January 1895 when 75 men and boys were entombed in the pit. On that fateful morning a great volume of underground water rushed towards them in a torrent described as 'three feet high'. William Dodd the Colliery Under-Manager received the Albert Medal from Queen Victoria at Windsor Castle on 9th March 1895 for his bravery in trying to rescue his men, others were recommended for the Royal Humane Society award.

In 1885 the mineworkers became more independent of the church and broke away, building their first school and chapel in Bignall End, called the Wesleyan Day School. This was only demolished in 1987 and a new modern school built on the site, preserving the foundation stone of the old school.

John Wedgwood, a squire of Bignall End who died in February 1839, declared in his will that he desired his body 'to be interred within my estate at Bignall End, in a vaulted tomb at the summit of a field called Old Hill, and an obelisk or monument to be erected'. The monument is still there, at some quarter of its original height, having been blown down in the severe gales of 1979, and never restored to its former height. It is situated on a most prominent spot, and is a familiar landmark as it can be seen for miles around.

Bishop's Wood 🦌

The land on which the village stands was given to the Bishop of Lichfield as a private hunting reserve in 1153 by King Henry II. The wood, predominantly oak, was still producing timber up to 1538. In the present day all that remains are four small woods or copses with names like Paradise Wood, Cream Pots, Pit Graves Hill, and Wet Hayes.

The Benedictine priory was established at Black Ladies by the Bishop of Lichfield, Roger de Clinton, in 1130. This was dissolved by King Henry VIII in 1538, and one year later purchased by the Gifford family of Chillington Hall in whose hands it remained until 1919. The orginal Norman buildings were replaced with a new priory in the early 16th century, and much of the fabric of that building is incorporated in the present house. In 1651 Black Ladies was garrisoned by Oliver Cromwell's men, who were searching the surrounding areas for King Charles II after the Battle at Worcester. Piercing the ricks of hay with their lances in their search they gave rise to the present day name of Pearce Hay Farm. The chapel at Black Ladies was in use for services until 1944.

In documents of 1680 Bishop's Wood was described as a little village consisting of a few scattered cottages encroaching onto the common land. This common was not enclosed until 1844. It was mainly a farming community with carpenters, blacksmith, wheelwright, shoemakers and other associated crafts. The area has long been noted for its damsons which were used for not only jam but also for dye in the First World War.

In the early 19th century, Miss Evans of Boscobel started two schools, one for Protestants and one for Roman Catholics: these were held in cottages at Park Pales and the common. In 1854 the first church school was built, three years after the church of St John the Evangelist. The present day altar was carved by a local craftsman Harry Onions in around 1950.

Bishop's Wood stands on what was once known as the highest tableland in the Midlands, and the base of the church is the same height as the spire of Brewood church. Uninterrupted views across to Cannock Chase to the east are enjoyed, and to the west can be seen the Wrekin. On the outskirts of the village is the Belvide Reservoir, widely recognised as a major bird reserve.

The present day village has changed in character, and with the building of some 200 houses in the early 1960s the population has increased to approximately 600. This necessitated the building of a new school, which was opened in 1969. There are still a number of working farms, although it is now more of a commuter village.

The Church Farm, originally called Church Stud Farm and Livery Stable, now has an arena which is on the National Show Jumping Circuit, and frequently sees top international riders, including Her Royal Highness The Princess Royal.

Blithfield 🌿

The parish of Blithfield, spelt Blidevelt in the Domesday Book, takes its name from the river Blythe and contained six original vills or manors. A village of Blithfield is said to have formerly existed near to the church, but this has long since disappeared and now the only remains are the Hall, church and rectory. The village merged with Stephens Hill and Admaston, it now being known by the latter, and Newton absorbed Hampton and Booth.

The church is dedicated to St Leonard and the oldest portion, the nave, most likely dates from the latter half of the 13th century. Mention is made in the Domesday Book of a priest of Blithfield which suggests that a church existed as early as 1086. North-west of the sanctuary is an elaborate monument commemorating Sir Lewis Bagot, three of his wives and his nineteen children. The Bagot family came to reside at the Hall in 1360 and for many years in the park in front of the house could be seen some of the Bagot goats which according to tradition were presented to Sir John Bagot by King Richard II in appreciation of the excellent hunting he had enjoyed in Bagots Park. A goats head is the Bagot family crest. Deer can also be found in areas known as Bagots Park and Bagots Wood.

In 1953 the river Blythe was dammed to form what is now known as Blithfield Reservoir and a farm amongst other properties vanished under the water. The South Staffordshire Waterworks own the reservoir which has trout hatcheries for the fishing which takes place and a sailing club. In the summer months people come to picnic at the side of the water. It is down the road leading over the reservoir that the Horn Dancers from the nearby village of Abbots Bromley make their way to Blithfield Hall each September to perform before Nancy, Lady Bagot who still resides there with her daughter.

In 1954 Blithfield rectory was divided into three large flats, but sadly, disaster struck in 1962 when fire destroyed the house leaving just an empty shell which is still standing today.

Sadly too, the village school, which served the parish and was situated at Admaston closed like many others in the early 1940s due to lack of numbers and the few remaining children were transported to a school in nearby Colton. The property belonged to the then Lord Bagot who gave it to the parish in 1945 to be used as a village hall.

At the other end of the parish lies Newton which consists mainly of two or three farms and old world cottages some of which have been transformed to present day standards. Although only a small part of the whole, Newton has been, as they say, 'put on the map' by virtue of its telephone box. A lady of the village Mrs Bertha Capewell has cleaned and polished the inside since the 1950s. Her efforts have received the attention of the media.

Bobbington 🌿

Bobbington is mentioned in the Domesday Book. It is quite a scattered parish but the village itself is linear in shape and there are approximately 500 inhabitants. The surrounding countryside is fields and mixed wood-lands, a very pleasant English landscape, not spectactular but rural agricultural land.

There is a church, chapel, school, village hall and a combined shop, post office and garage, as well as an airfield at Halfpenny Green, built by the Air Ministry in 1939.

The church was originally called St Mary's but in 1905 when it was brought back into the Lichfield Diocese it was rededicated to The Holy Cross. It is 11th century, with Norman arches and pillars but the bases of the two narrow end pillars adjoining the walls are Saxon, no doubt part of an earlier Saxon church, once built on the same site. In the church today, is a plaque commemorating the death of HRH Prince William of Gloucester, killed in an aircrash at the Goodyear Air Race in August 1972 at the Halfpenny Green Airfield. There is a wrought-iron flower stand, given by HRH Princess Alice, Duchess of Gloucester in memory of Prince William.

The chapel, opened in 1883, was built on a corner of Bill's Piece, formerly on Bobbington Common, though there is another old building which was used as the first Dissenting Chapel, built in 1830 on the edge of the Common.

While at one time all the villagers would have been employed in agricultural work, this has slowly changed over the years. Even in the 1950s, there was a sprinkling of people travelling into the surrounding towns for employment. New houses have been built for sale since the

1960s and this has seen townspeople coming into the country to live, making Bobbington more of a commuter village.

At one time, Bobbington had a rural industry known as Bobbington Mills or by the local population as the 'Grass Dryers', which eventually became Everest Frozen Foods, where a number of local people found regular employment. This has now gone to larger premises in a nearby larger village but the old buildings are still used by them as stores.

The original vicarage was a spacious Victorian house, in a large garden with adjoining glebeland, next door to the church. This was sold and modern houses were built on the land. A fairly new house on the opposite side of the road was bought for a vicarage and is now occupied by a lay minister.

The village hall was built after the war and was a wooden structure. Many activities have taken place there and still do. It has been enlarged and modernized over the years.

Bobbington had its first Church of England school in 1792, founded by the sisters Hannah and Mary Corbett. This school was replaced in 1892 by a school at White Cross. This was demolished in 1944 because it was in the flight path from Halfpenny Green Airfield and moved to its present site.

Bradnop ∉

Bradnop lies in the Staffordshire Moorlands, 2½ miles south-east of Leek, on the road to Ashbourne, a world away from the lowland towns and industrial south of the county.

Driving along the main road, one would be unaware of the existence of the village. Turning left at the crossroad you are in School Lane, leading to what was the heart of the village. Children came to school from very far afield, Bradnop being such a scattered area. Sparsely populated, with about 350 persons, Bradnop consists mainly of isolated farms and cottages, many of them over a mile from the road.

This is a strong Non-Conformist area, and the Wesleyan chapel was built in 1834. Services are still held here regularly.

As there was no Anglican church, when the school was built in 1862, it was licensed for church worship, with the vicar of Onecote-cum-Bradnop officiating.

Bradnop has lost a lot in the last few years. The village school closed in 1978. At one time there was a Primitive Methodist chapel, built in 1889, closed in 1970. There was a public house, wheelwright and blacksmith, also a post office. Now, not even a telephone kiosk. There was a railway station. The line still exists to carry stone from Cauldon Lowe quarries to the main line at Stoke. The last passenger train was in 1935. Three houses were built, in brick, for railway staff, and these are the only 'attached' houses in the village.

Apart from a very few new houses, all buildings are in grey gritstone. As the elevation is between 800 to 1000 feet above sea level, these would be built from local stone to withstand the elements. Stone walls outnumber hedges.

There is evidence that many of the local houses (present structures being about 200 years old) have been built on much older foundations.

Farming is still the mainstay. It must have been a very hard life trying to make a living from the land, much of it now designated as hill farm, or marginal land, when there was no electricity, no piped water, no telephones, and not many cars. There is still no main sewerage system. Yet people survived, reared large families, and very rarely moved out of the locality.

Bramshall & Loxley 🌿

Bramshall is situated between the market town of Uttoxeter and Loxley. The main Derby to Crewe railway-line runs near by. The village has a post office/shop and two public houses. The Butchers Arms is situated on the main Uttoxeter to Stone road and the Robin Hood, once known as The New Inn, near Dagdale Lane, on the Bramshall to Leigh road. There is also a butcher's shop. Together the oak beamed farmhouses and cottages, scenic views and the new housing estate make Bramshall a picturesque and delightful village.

The original church of St Lawrence was built in the reign of Edward III, although there may once have been an even earlier one. It was a simple building with a tower at the west end. In 1834 it was found to be in a dangerous condition, so it was pulled down and the present building erected on similar lines. Fortunately a drawing was made of the old church before it was destroyed. Two medieval bells, the Caroline altar rails, and some 14th and 16th century glass have survived from the old church.

Bramshall church was rebuilt in the year 1835 by Lord Willoughy de Broke. It stands on an eminence above the village and is a plain Gothic stone building with a low embattled tower, having three bells. It possesses some of the most interesting stained glass in this district.

Loxley, situated two miles along the Uttoxeter to Stafford Road was the former estate of the Sneyd-Kynnersley family. The first of the estate sales took place in 1918.

The Hall, rebuilt in 1792 dominates the area of scattered farms and cottages. Carved stonework from the old Hall depicting the family coat of arms was used for the front of a folly in Long Walk Wood known as Robin Hood's chapel. According to legend Robin Hood often visited Loxley. A vase, found in the park was used by Sir Josiah Wedgwood as a model. He made 26 copies and called it the Loxley vase.

A memorial stone in one of the fields marks the spot where Craven Sneyd-Kynnersley, aged 23, was accidently shot in 1735.

During the Second World War the Hall was occupied by prisoners of war and American servicemen. Highfields Hall, the Dearndales and Loxley Bank Farm were sold in 1945.

Finally the Hall itself was bought by the Staffordshire Education Committee for use as a school.

Branston ✿

Pickle lovers everywhere have heard of Branston, but few of them know anything about it. It is a friendly village with a population of almost 3,000 by the river Trent just south of Burton, which brews the ale to go with the pickle!

Change is the keyword in describing Branston, whose modern appearance is deceptive. Driving out of Burton, houses line the A5121 in ribbon development style and you hardly notice that you have entered the village before you are through it and out along the A38 by-pass. Slow up a little and look around and you will discover a few clues to its long and varied history.

A long high wall protects 'the Depot' – now used for Home Office

Supplies. It began as the National Machine Gun Factory in 1915, and was the pickle factory for four years in the 1920s, before producing artificial silk. It now houses, among other things, the 'Green Goddess' fire-tenders used in emergencies.

Across the road is Paget High School built in 1973, a reminder that the village has had a succession of owners – the Saxon thane, Eadwig, Lady Godiva, Burton Abbey and Sir William Paget and his descendants, the Marquises of Anglesey. For centuries, Branston was a farming community when large herds grazed the rich, well-drained meadows by the river Trent. Today, only Lawns Farm remains as a working farm, though neighbouring farmers till other fields.

St Saviour's church, dating from 1864, was given a 'face lift' in 1981 with the addition of a gabled meeting room, a new porch and toilets. In 1985, the vicar and his family moved into a new house at the bottom of his garden and the old vicarage became a select eating-house. The United Reformed church, formerly Congregational, built in 1834 has closed.

The long brick wall on Main Street surrounded the gardens of Branston Hall, a neo-classical residence demolished in the 1960s when the houses and bungalows of Leamington Road were built.

In 1845, children went to school in an old cowshed on Church Road, and then the school moved to a new building in 1874 next to the Blacksmith's Arms. This was rebuilt a few yards to the right in 1964 to make way for the A38 approach road. It is called Ryknild School after the Roman road, which went through the village, linking Worcester and York.

The river's course has moved slightly near Trent House, which is now the popular Riverside Inn restaurant and motel, and a strong bank protects the village from the floods it used to suffer. One public house has closed – the Anglesey Arms on Main Street – but the rest are thriving. The Bridge Inn with its pretty gardens by the Trent and Mersey canal is popular with those touring in narrow boats. The Blacksmith's Arms stands next to the site of the old forge, and the Gate Inn marks the old entrance to the village before the by-pass was made.

Parallel with the canal is Branston Pool, near the old gravel workings, enjoyed by birdwatchers and windsurfers, fishermen and walkers.

Brewood 🦢

Over 50 years ago hiring a rowing boat on the canal at Brewood was quite the thing to do. People came out from the towns to participate and to picnic. Now the canal, which hugs the edge of the village, is alive with more commercial enterprises. A whole smart fleet of canal boats stands in readiness for holiday hires.

The village itself has several smart Georgian houses and a varied and interesting centre. One of the unusual pieces of architecture is 'Speedwell castle'. It is the only Grade I listed residence in Brewood, described as Georgian Gothic. The name 'Speedwell', it is believed, came from a horse of that name, presumably the winnings paid for the building!

Chillington Hall, south-west of the village is the home of the Giffards. Theirs is a long and interesting family history. The house and part of the extensive grounds are open from May until September on Thursday afternoons, well worth a visit.

The parish church of St Mary and St Chad, which in parts dates back to the 12th century, is surrounded by an ancient and well kept graveyard. The headstones tell their own story of the old Brewood families, lots of whom still carry on in the village to-day. West of the village is the Roman Catholic church of St Mary, completed in 1844. It was designed by Pugin, who was responsible for much interior detail of the Houses of Parliament. A small but well used Methodist chapel is wedged in School Street, between houses. It is well worth searching out.

Below the chapel on the corner of Newport Street is an old frame house known as The Mansion. Behind it hides the restored locksmith's cottage. Lockmaking has its roots in Brewood. If history had taken a different turn and Brewood had been better served by the railways, Brewood would have been an industrial town and Willenhall (now the heart of the lock industry) would have been merely a quiet village.

In Bargate Street is Bargate House, where a past owner must have been concerned about the window tax, as there are several bricked-in windows on the facade. This house was once a toll house, as was the chemist shop in the Square. Now its fame is proclaimed by a plaque which commemorates Walker the engineer.

Off Sandy Lane is Jacobs Ladder, a flight of worn steps which lead to the back of the churchyard and straight through to Deans Street, a street of well kept interesting houses, mostly Georgian. The importance of the village's past reveals itself in the house names in the street: The Deanery, Deans Cottage etc.

Brewood is a busy village with good shops and a new library. There is somewhere to rest one's tired feet. Most of the pubs serve food, and a pot of tea and home made cakes are always available at Studio One on week-days. A full guide book can be purchased in the village.

Brocton ⚘

Brocton is a small, attractive and popular residential village situated on the edge of Cannock Chase. In 1958 Cannock Chase was designated as an Area of Outstanding Natural Beauty, with a total extent of 26 square miles. It consists of heather and bracken covered hills and open spaces, as well as Forestry Commission woodlands and remnants of ancient oak woodlands.

As one stands on the village green today, it is hard to visualise the present residential properties as they were in the past. The cottage now called The Fentons was, until 1927, a working blacksmith's and the original post office was at the bottom of Chase Road. The present boutique was a general store with the undertaker at the rear. The school room was at one time in the black and white cottage and there were also two butchers. The present church was opened as a Mission Room in 1891 and was also used as a school room before it was dedicated to All Saints in 1950. The church is open daily. Brocton Farm, just a little further away on the same side used to have its own herd of cows and supplied milk to the village.

A short way from the village green, on Sawpit Lane, is Brocton Hall, originally the home of the Chetwynd family who owned much of Brocton. It is now a well known golf club (reputed to be haunted by a grey lady) with a picturesque 18 hole course. A visit to the local pub, named after the Chetwynd family, on Cannock Road, could complete a walk in this direction.

Along Old Acre Lane is the present village hall, the centre for many village activities. Beyond the end of the lane is Brocton Nature Reserve, where a lake formed by the flooding of the former Brocton gravel quarry is the home of a variety of birds which can be viewed from a hide.

Chase Road leads to the site of Brocton Camp, a First World War army training camp. On Chase Road can be seen the glacial boulder, a landmark, which is on the site of the Brocton Camp water tower. The boulder was found in Brocton quarry and had been carried from South-West Scotland during the Ice Age.

One popular walk is to Brocton Coppice where ancient oaks can be found. These are the last remnant of the natural forest which existed before charcoal burning took place on a large scale. The present day Cannock Chase forms part of what was once a vast hunting ground known as the King's Forest of Cannock where King Henry II hunted deer and other game. Small areas in the Coppice have been fenced off and replanted to replace the ancient oaks which seem unable to regenerate themselves due to the large number of animals who eat the acorns, and the deer who eat the young trees. Fallow deer were introduced to the Chase about 1,000 years ago and an ancient herd, numbering about 250 still roam the Chase.

The common at Milford, a popular venue for motorists, is only 1½ miles away and here most facilities are available together with the Chase Information Office. Here booklets, maps and guides relating to various aspects of Cannock Chase can be purchased. Across the common is the entrance to Shugborough Hall, the ancestral home of the Earls of Lichfield. The present Earl, Patrick Lichfield, and his sister Elizabeth still have a residence here. This stately home is open to the public and is under the care of the National Trust. The Staffordshire County Museum and the Home Farm specialising in rare breeds are within the estate and can be visited.

Broughton 🦋

Broughton is situated on the B5026 between Eccleshall and Loggerheads and there are several marvellous buildings here which make the village well worth a visit.

St Peter's church was built in the 1630s and retains many original features, such as high box pews. It also contains monuments to the Broughton family from the 17th and 18th centuries.

The home of the Broughton family, Broughton Hall, stands opposite the church and, as Nikolaus Pevsner says, is the 'most spectacular piece of black and white in the county'. The exterior is dated 1637 and is wonderfully decorated, three storeys high and with overhanging upper storeys.

This beautiful house is said to be haunted by a ghost known as 'Red Socks'. A woman from the village was scrubbing the Long Gallery attic stairs one day when she was conscious of someone standing above her. She looked up and saw a young man, in red stockings, about to descend the stairs. She got up and moved her bucket to one side to let him pass, but to her horror he walked right through her. She continued to do her cleaning in the Long Gallery after that, but took care to always have a companion with her.

Charnes Hall is an early Georgian building just off the B5026 and for many years the home of the Vernon Yonge family. It has been in the ownership of the Hall family since 1916. This house too has a ghost, seen by many people over the past 200 years. She is a lady known as 'Silkie', said to be looking for a lost ring which was stolen from her by a servant as she lay in her tomb!

Brown Edge 🐑

Situated in the northern part of Staffordshire, Brown Edge was built on one of the south westerly spurs of the Pennine Chain, its highest point, Hill Top, being 920 feet above sea level. It is a small compact hamlet which came into existence with the development of coal mining in the area. Old history books describe it as 'cold and hilly' and 'poor stony land', and it is thought the 'Brown' in the name refers to this poor, uncultivated land. However, land on the west slopes to the river Trent and is good agricultural land with farmhouses dating from about 1600 and still farmed today.

Until the Industrial Revolution there were few inhabitants, but the population grew with the opening of local mines. The miners built cottages on the wasteland, often without permission from the Lords of Norton.

However, the village remained isolated with no railway station, a primitive sewage system and no piped water. As a result of this isolation

45

the miners formed a friendly, close-knit community, many families having nicknames such as Backers, Pell, Flick and Pup. They had different talents, consequently they provided their own entertainment. St Anne's church was built in 1844 and there was also a strong Chapel movement. A branch of the YMCA was formed, a football and hockey team, bellringers and a Horticultural Society.

In 1921 something occurred which helped to bring about the end of the village's isolation. Samuel Turner purchased a Ford one-ton chassis, built a body in the form of a charabanc with a canvas top and began his reliable bus service.

St Anne's church school was built in 1845 and was of a poor standard until 1880 when Mr William Jones, headmaster for 40 years, transformed it to a model school. Mrs Benton, a former pupil teacher who later qualified and taught at Endon Senior School, was awarded the MBE for good work in education.

The village has changed with some new property and increased traffic along its narrow roads. At one time there were many small shops around

The old Schoolmaster's House at Brown Edge

the village, but now there are nine centred around the main road. The two butchers and the two supermarkets are old family businesses. There are no more sing-songs at The Foaming Quart as it was re-opened as Varsovia Lodge, a first class restaurant. St Anne's school was closed, in a bad state of repair, but the villagers raised money for the historic building to be converted to a village hall. Turner's bus service was run by the family until 31st October 1987 when, sadly, it was bought out.

Burntwood 🐝

Burntwood used to be a typical Staffordshire village with its inhabitants being mainly employed in agriculture, in the coal mines of the adjoining villages, at the local psychiatric hospital or, many years ago, in nail making. It is not that many years ago that the hospital, now known as St Matthew's Hospital, was more or less self supporting. It had its own gas works, electricity plant, bakery, laundry and a farm and gardens which provided the majority of the potatoes and vegetables for use in the hospital and also some rehabilitation for the patients.

Burntwood had, and still has, its fair share of inns and pubs with The Swan really being the focal point of the old village centre because of its position. When the local mines first started in the mid 19th century The Swan used to open its doors at 5 am so that miners could get a drink on their way to work! Not surprisingly in later years this practice ceased.

The village has one or two residences of some note. On the edge of the parish stands a mansion known as Maple Hayes. It was sold in 1949 and used as a boarding house attached to King Edward VI grammar school in Lichfield but it is now a specialised school for dyslexic children. At Maple Hayes Dr Erasmus Darwin, the famous botanist, founded his botanical gardens.

The other residence worthy of note and built about 1680–1700 is Edial Hall. For a short time this was the home of Dr Samuel Johnson and it was here that he opened a school where 'young gentlemen are boarded and taught Latin and Greek languages'.

In the early 1960s planners and builders alike singled Burntwood out as one of those places ripe for expansion and almost overnight new housing estates were going up in its green fields. New schools, supermarkets, shops, garages and an industrial estate followed. The building is still going on as new 'executive homes' go up and the green belt gets pushed further and further out. Whilst the loss of the old country lifestyle is regretted, 'old' Burntwood residents have been keen to move into the newer houses and take full advantage of the better facilities.

Some years ago the 'powers-that-be' decided that Burntwood and her adjoining villages of Chasetown and Chase Terrace had all grown so much that they should be amalgamated and designated a town under the collective name of Burntwood. This was duly carried out, but each village is still fiercely protective of its own identity and the old and new inhabitants of Burntwood village suddenly found themselves with a common cause – to protect 'their' Burntwood.

Butterton 🐑

The village of Butterton is of ancient foundation. In Saxon times the Lyme Forest covered the area and clearings were made to create a settlement at Butterton together with adjoining settlements at Trentham, Acton and Keele.

The size of the village, as measured by the number of families in the community and the area of land under cultivation, grew progressively until the 13th century but it was clearly in decline again by the 16th century when the Swinnerton family acquired land at Butterton and built the Old Hall in 1540. In the 17th and 18th centuries the Swinnertons progressively enlarged their estate in and around Butterton converting it in the process into a Park. A new and much larger Butterton Hall was built in 1850 and the Old Hall was demolished apart from a small section which, ruined and ivy-covered, stands to this day. Ownership of the estate had passed by marriage to the Pilkington family by this time and they built the church, dedicated to St Thomas, in 1845. A school was built in Butterton village in 1871 which became the centre of a hamlet previously known as Millstone Green.

Butterton Hall was demolished in 1921, some of the stone being re-used, the most interesting example being the Club House of Newcastle Golf Club. The school was closed in 1968 the children being transferred to the school at Baldwin's Gate. St Thomas' church – 'the Church in the fields' – alone remains standing and is in regular use.

Historically Butterton was initially a farming community but the development of the estate meant that estate-workers progressively dominated. It is interesting to note, however, that other types of work existed, as for example home-working shoemakers at Millstone Green who worked for shoe manufacturers in Stone and glove making at the Lymes Farm.

The appearance of Butterton has changed little in the last 100 years apart from the building of seven houses following the breaking up of the estate in 1954. The 'Spout' which was the main source of drinking water still runs and never goes dry. The Victorian post box built into a house wall and the school building, boarded up and overgrown, still remain as monuments to the old way of life. The community of today is largely employed in towns within commuting distance of the village but farming is still carried on at the Lymes Farm, New Hayes Farm and Butterton Grange. Butterton Nurseries operate on the site of the walled kitchen garden of the Old Hall.

An interesting geological feature of the area is the Butterton Dyke, an igneous intrusion which runs close to the church along the line of a belt of trees.

Canwell

Canwell lies in the south of the county, with houses and farms scattered in a haphazard way over rolling hills, fields and woods. The only semblance of a village is where the school, some houses, a farm, and a Social Hall cluster near a crossroads, only about half a mile from the boundary with what is now the West Midlands. No village street, no village green! Very dispersed and strewn around is Canwell, which consequently rather lacks a sense of unity and a feeling of togetherness.

Canwell goes back to the Middle Ages, when there was a priory, but no village. The priory was founded in 1142 and had strong links with the manor of Drayton.

Eventually Sir Francis Lawley bought the estate and Canwell remained in the Lawley's possession from 1700 to 1872. The family built a Hall, and stables were built from the ruins of the priory. An elementary school was established in 1851. In 1872 the Hall and estate was sold to A B

Foster, when there were 193 people living in Canwell, and 38 houses. Most, if not all the people worked at the Hall or on the estate. A B Foster's son, Philip, enlarged and supported the school and it was called the Philip Foster school. Sadly the school was closed in the early 1980s, as was the post office and the only shop. But happily, at the end of 1987 a flourishing nursery school was opened in part of the old school.

Canwell church, built in 1911 as a private chapel to the Hall by the Fosters, is a small, quite delightful Early English style building, beautifully built and maintained, although the congregation is scattered over many miles.

Then in 1920, something happened which completely changed this quiet, peaceful part of South Staffordshire. Birmingham City Council bought the Hall and 25 surrounding acres, sold off 250 acres of unsuitable land and divided the remaining land into small-holdings for ex-service men, part of a Goverment Land Settlement Scheme. Today, many houses have been sold, land redistributed so that farms are larger and, while there are still tenants, many have bought their own farms.

The Hall with its 25 surrounding acres was used as a convalescent home for soldiers, but principally as a childrens hospital. This hospital goes down in history as the first one in England to use penicillin. The hospital was closed the day before the Coronation in 1953, when Little Bromwich Hospital had been opened. Canwell Hall was pulled down in 1958.

Canwell holds an annual Agricultural Show, which from modest beginnings in 1925, is now one of the largest one day shows, with entries from far and wide.

To end on rather a gruesome note. There is a steep hill where now runs the main road to Tamworth and beyond. This road is wooded, but not so densely as in earlier times, when even on a sunny day it was dark. This is called Carroway Head, but legend has it that it was once called Gallows Way Head, where stood a gibbet, which travellers on their journeyings had to pass. Imagine on a dark night, the sound of creakings, and sinister shapes swinging in the wind!

Caverswall 🌿

The naming of the village seems to derive from the original inhabitant Cafhere, who found a spring and called his settlement Cafhere's Walle or Cafhere's Spring.

In 1066 the village consisted of a cluster of small houses, the church was a small stone building and the castle, a modest Saxon hall.

There have been various extensions to the church and castle over the centuries. Observing the church from the south side these can be noted from the 11th century through to the Victorian era.

The castle, originally a Saxon hall, was developed over the ensuing centuries until in the early 17th century the present day castle was constructed, and portions of the earlier building restored. The exterior of the building retains all the features of a Jacobean mansion house.

During the Norman period successive Lords of the Manor developed the village community, notably Walter and William de Kaverswalle. A memorial to both lies in St Peter's church today.

In the 14th century the Black Death struck the village. Rumour has it that this had some part to play in the present churchyard being raised well above the adjacent road, but in reality this actually shows the direct consequence of burying in one place over a long period of time.

The village still has stocks in the square, ornamental today, but in the 16th century beggars would be pelted by the excited villagers as they were feared and abhored by all. The square also provided a centre for bloody sports such as bull baiting and cock fighting as well as the quieter pastimes of singing and dancing.

In 1811 20 Benedictine nuns purchased the castle for £4,000 to provide a quiet and secluded home where they ran a boarding school for young Catholic ladies for 30 guineas per annum. The local people regarded these secretive sisters with suspicion because of their apparent growing wealth. In 1853, partly for economic reasons, the sisters left Caverswall. Before leaving they destroyed their chapel and all that remained of those nuns who died whilst at Caverswall.

The castle has since been occupied by two different sets of nuns. The last group ran a guest home for elderly ladies, but left Caverswall in 1977, when the castle was sold in various lots. It is to the credit of these people that the castle maintains its original beauty, although not available for public viewing.

A memory of olden days is to be seen on the sign of the village public house, The Red House, which consists of a 'merry go round' with the words 'Rum Tum Tardy um' around the top. These words are taken from an old song thought to have started life as a marching song for the Caverswall volunteers during the Napoleonic Wars.

The village, which is protected by a conservation order, remains a virtual backwater and remote from surrounding villages. True, there is a twice daily surge of traffic as the village offers a network of minor roads to the five towns of Stoke-on-Trent, but being mainly agricultural it remains calm during the day.

Chapel Chorlton 🌿

Chapel Chorlton is a small village some 6½ miles south-west of New-castle-under-Lyme. There is a church, village green, five farms, and a number of houses stretched along the ridge of a range of hills.

The village green is triangular in shape; in the centre an oak tree stands, planted to commemorate Queen Victoria's Golden Jubilee. Alongside the green is a pool, well-known to visitors for fishing, which has been landscaped to retain its character. On the other side of the green there are the remains of an old penfold.

In the fields surrounding the village, green sandstone was quarried and the stone used for local buildings. During the construction of the M6 motorway these stone quarries were filled with surplus material from the excavations, so all trace of them has now been lost.

The church of St Laurence is of Norman origin and was built of local stone. The register dates from 1564. There are indications that the church has been rebuilt a number of times, the last time in the year 1827. It consists of a nave and a western tower with four pinnacles. The ancient bell bears the inscription 'Ave Maria gratia plena Dominus tecum' – the date probably 16th century. There is an oak pulpit of Jacobean date.

Nearby there was a National School, which was built in the year 1848 and enlarged in 1871 to cater for 50 children. It continued in existence until the 1970s. The school building has now been converted into a dwelling house.

The Lord of the Manor, and principal landowner during the last century, was Sir Delves Broughton. The farms have since been sold. The date of the old manor house is uncertain, but it is believed to have been built in the 17th century. For many years it was used as a boys boarding school. In the main large school room the oak beams bear the scorch marks of the oil lamps.

Chasetown ৶৵৹

Chasetown is a village of coal-mining origins: the High Street, unhurried and friendly, is its hub. The small family-owned shops, dwellings and public houses are a blend of Victorian and Edwardian properties, built in a simple functional style, reflecting the needs of the early coal-mining era.

The name Chasetown is self-explanatory, 'The Chase' being the extensive hunting grounds of King Henry II upon which the village developed.

Much of the commonland and farmland in the Chasetown area formerly belonged to the Marquess of Anglesey and, but for a few farms, the land was unpopulated. The opening of the Cannock Chase Coalfield must have caused the Marquess to ponder upon the hidden wealth lying beneath his land, prompting him to sink two pits in Chasetown in 1849 and 1852.

When in 1854 the mines were leased to John Robinson McLean (later MP for East Staffordshire) and Richard Croft Chawner, Chairman of the South Staffordshire Waterworks Company, there began a period of intensive growth in coal production. These entrepreneurs formed the Cannock Chase Colliery Company in 1859, extending their mining interests by sinking a further eight pits in nearby villages.

John McLean proved to be a great benefactor to Chasetown, founding St Anne's church, a beautiful red and blue brick building, executed inside in neo-Byzantine style. It claims the distinction of being the first church to be lit by electricity, which was supplied by 'The Fly' colliery generator. During periods of heavy rain, water seeped below ground and the heat generated by this early form of electric supply caused steam to rise from the pavement, much to the alarm of passers by.

Chasetown village was the beneficiary of both welfare and recreational facilities; the company financed a school, mining institute, village institute, sportsfield and recreation ground.

Sadly when the mining industry was nationalised in 1947 only four of the company's collieries were operational and when those too, not being viable, had ceased production by 1961 it seemed that the raison d'etre for Chasetown had vanished.

Coal is no longer the predominant source of employment but village miners still travel to super-pits outside the area and the development of local industrial estates provides a wider variety of jobs.

Chasetown retains a strong village identity despite the fact that steady growth has culminated in the merging of three villages, Chasetown, Chaseterrace and Burntwood to form the urban parish of Burntwood.

Legacies of the mining era are fast disappearing and the spoil tips at the end of Church Street have undergone a remarkable transformation. Funded by the Department of the Environment, they are now pleasantly-contoured, tree-planted, clover-fragrant, poolside walks and Chasewater reservoir is a venue for all types of water pursuits.

Cheddleton 🌿

Two names spring to mind when Cheddleton is mentioned – the Flint Mill and Brittains' Paper Mill. The latter alas no longer functions, but the Flint Mill is still a favourite haunt of visitors to the Staffordshire Moorlands. With its two waterwheels, the mill is known far and wide, and its setting between the canal and river Churnet is lovely indeed.

St Edward the Confessor church in the old village is a most beautiful sacred building, having William Morris stained glass windows, benefactions boards well worth reading, and a truly peaceful atmosphere. Near to the priest's door in the churchyard is a tombstone marked N.T. 1679. The old pound is a few yards distant from the church.

In years gone by the Quaker movement had members in Cheddleton, and there is an old Quaker burial ground near to Basford Hall. Whitehough, an old manor farmhouse situated between Cheddleton and Ipstones had strong Quaker connections.

Near to St Edward's church is the oldest inhabited site, with stocks on the church wall facing on to the Black Lion Inn. Another old inn, the Red Lion in Cheadle Road, with the Boat Inn at the entrance to the Churnet valley, ensure that Cheddleton is well supplied with places of refreshment and relaxation.

Cheddleton has other historic places, including the railway station and museum, the station building itself being designed by Pugin. With the help of the late Sir John Betjeman this gem was saved from destruction.

Ashcombe Park Cricket ground is in a delightful spot, overlooking the Churnet valley and the most beautiful scenery towards Ipstones. The recently opened Community Centre is the venue for Parish Council and Women's Institute meetings, and the discussion of all and sundry matters arising from village life.

Chesterton & Apedale

Apedale estate is an area on the outskirts of Chesterton, with a history stretching back to the days of the Romans. The estate was large and consisted in Chesterton of lands called Roggin, Glasshouse and Beasley. Land in the area is known to have remains of Roman occupation and for a number of years archaeological excavations were carried out on Whitehouse Farm.

The estate belonged to the Greasley family until Sir John Edensor Heathcote married Anne Greasley in 1780, the Heathcotes then becoming Lords of the Manor. Both Chesterton and nearby Alsagers Bank have cause to be grateful for the generosity of the family over the years.

A works opened in 1785 making iron ore, believed to be the first iron ore furnace in England. Until the 1930s this was a busy industrial and coal mining area. A reminder of the dangers involved still stands as a memorial to the Burley Pit disaster – a chimney bearing on all four sides the words:

> Live and let live
> Regard the end
> Be just and fear not.

In 1785 the Eagle and Child inn was built as a coaching inn and is still used today. Chesterton continued to grow and the parish church of Holy Trinity was built in 1852. The story goes that a man by the name of Sneyd said he would give the stone for the church if on a certain day in

July it rained. Needless to say, it rained without ceasing for 48 hours. The estate was sold in 1931. Various small businesses carried on, such as sawmills. Now opencast mining seems set to alter the beautiful valley of Apedale once again.

Chorley & Farewell

Chorley is some three to four miles from Lichfield, a small village nestling between fields of sheep and cows, with winding narrow lanes.

Chorley and Farewell are mainly farming communities. Some of the homes have been in one family for two or three generations. The Hammersleys, of Hill Farm have farmed the area for many years, passed on from father to son.

Chorley has some lovely old houses. Lodge Farm dating back to 1737, still has servants' quarters and a back stair. Once the home of the squire, in summer, cream teas were served to passers-by.

Farewell Hall and church, are beautiful old places of local interest, the church dating back to 1140. Cross-in-hand Lane leads to St Bartholomew's church. It is believed that travellers seeking sanctuary would take this lane, bearing a cross, hence the name. 'God is Love' above the church door was carved by Mr Jack Ball, a villager.

The original school was a typical village school, with large fires and just two teachers for varying ages of children. In bygone days, children were often absent in winter, some having no suitable footwear. In summer boys went to work in the fields, or if measles hit the village numbers would also be low. The school was also used for a number of other events ie, dances, plays etc. It now maintains its character and charm as a private house.

In 1961 a new school, Fairley, was erected and opened opposite the old. As the years rolled on and people moved away children became fewer and in 1983 the school was closed, a very sad day indeed. There now stand two houses on the site.

The Malt Shovel Inn has featured highly in village life for over fifty years. Many disputes as to who has grown the biggest onions at the annual horticultural show, or whose pigeons haven't returned, have been solved over a pint beside the roaring fire. Today's Malt Shovel is popular with visitors during summertime.

Codsall ✤

If you travel only a short distance from the Midlands and are asked where you live, the reply 'Codsall, near Wolverhampton' invariably sets the enquirer visualising factory chimneys, heavy industry and grime. Not so! Codsall is set in 'green and pleasant land' a short walk from the Shropshire border. While not so attractive in appearance as it was some 30 years ago, many of its old cottages and elegant houses having been demolished in the interests of commerce and so called progress, it still retains a village atmosphere and is not merely a dormitory suburb of Wolverhampton.

Prior to the 1960s keen gardeners were familiar with Codsall as the home of Baker's Nurseries, where the multi-coloured Russell lupins were first grown in 1935, as was the Bishop delphinium. Indeed, the Baker family who owned the nurseries lived for many years in the house in Church Road that was the birthplace of Sir Charles Wheeler KCVO the well known President of the Royal Academy, 1956–66. Prior to the 1950s a large proportion of the village, male and female, worked at the nurseries, growing the plants, packing the seeds etc. Then the business was transferred to nearby Boningale and ultimately ceased to exist. Mr James Baker the owner, was a director of Wolverhampton Wanderers Football Club for many years.

In 1086 only six people were recorded as living in Codsall. In 1327 eleven were assessed for tax in the locality, but by 1971 the population had increased to 9,027 and is now some 12,000 – a veritable population explosion. In the 1940s Codsall ceased to be a home only for those employed in agriculture or domestic service and began to develop into a residential area, although the Bull Inn existed in 1791 surrounded, as such hostelries usually were, by a cluster of cottages. In 1850 the Great Western Railway opened the station, roads began to radiate from the hub of the village and Victorian 'commuters' began to build and buy properties in increasing numbers.

Curiously, Codsall church is not situated in the village centre but stands a little way out at the top of a long incline and is the highest point between here and Russia, a fact to which shivering communicants climbing the hill on a winter morning will testify. The view from the churchyard is magnificent, for on a clear day, looking north-west and away from the main residential areas the distant Wrekin and Welsh mountains can be seen beyond a pastel patchwork of fields and small woods. Also visible is the path to what was once the Leper Well and the crossroads where an unfortunate unnamed female was hanged.

Codsall offers its residents a wide variety of interesting societies and clubs for their leisure, while three excellent public houses offer good food and good ale.

Codsall Wood ✑

Codsall Wood is a hamlet of about 150 people on the edge of the large parish of Codsall, about 7 miles north-west of Wolverhampton. For centuries most of Codsall Wood was the common (or waste) land within the manor of the Deanery of the Collegiate church of Wolverhampton. The common was enclosed in 1824 under a special Act of Parliament and the area was divided up into plots which form the basis of the present-day housing and the two inns.

Codsall Wood has its own church, post office, village shop, the Crown Inn and the Cross Guns Inn. These were all established in the 19th century when there were also three other inns – the Old Giffards, the New Giffards and the Crow in the Wood. There were several hovels around the edge of the common land in which farm workers, woodmen and labourers lived.

Wood Hall Farm was once moated and can be traced back to the 13th century. The Stockings and Husphins Farms are centuries old and there is Dead Woman's Grave. Pendrell Hall is now the County Council's College for adult education and takes students from all over the country. There used to be a smithy, which is now a car workshop, and a wheelwright's shop.

For 40 years the village of Codsall Wood has run a very popular Flower Show and Garden competition which has raised substantial sums for charity.

Traditionally villagers do not live 'at Codsall Wood' but 'on Codsall Wood'. The houses are a mixture of restored cottages and modern residences. Many of the residents still work locally in the pubs, the shop, the post office, the local builder's yard and in home industries.

The M54 runs close to Codsall Wood. Whilst this new motorway has been cleverly landscaped to be visually inoffensive, that bonus has been lost by the use of a very noisy road surface. But for the successful opposition of the villagers, the motorway might have been ruinously near to the hamlet. Otherwise surrounded by farm lands the village is almost 500 feet above sea level with views to Cannock Chase, the Wrekin and the Clee Hills. It is bordered by the ancient Chillington estate of the Giffard family with its lake, bridges, temples and Capability Brown landscape.

Colton 🌿

On entering Colton the first point of interest is the Brook Bridge with its four large boulders, one at each of the bridge walls, which are glacial in origin.

The Domesday Survey records 'The Priest of Colton' in the year 1086, and the parish church of St Mary the Virgin has a list of rectors dating from that year until 1977. The church was largely rebuilt in the 19th century but traces of much older buildings remain. It is interesting to note that in 1270 a murderer took sanctuary here, one Nicholas, son of William de Colton, who stabbed Adam the son of Hereward in a brawl and fled into the church for refuge.

Present day villagers are much involved every two years in organising Festival weekends for the benefit of the church and the building of a new village hall.

Colton House, built probably in the reign of Queen Anne, is believed to occupy the site of a Saxon timber-built manor in which resided a lord named Azeline, a man of considerable importance. A 17th century thrashing barn removed from Parchfields Farm, has been restored and re-erected at Wolseley Bridge and is now an attractive antique and craft centre.

The High House, as its name implies, is a building of considerable height. The upper storeys are lived in as a private dwelling, but the ground floor houses the village general store and post office.

The first school in Colton goes back over 200 years when villagers subscribed for a number of poor children to have some basic education. The present school was built in 1862, and was improved and extended in 1967.

Belamore (or Bellamour) Hall was built in 1635 by Herbert Aston, son of Sir Walter Aston, Ambassador to Spain. It was said to have been haunted by the widow of a man who was murdered at the Hall.

There were many charities for parishioners, providing benefits such as a threepenny loaf weekly for 12 widows, a long thick black coat for men, a red flannel petticoat for women, a substantial dinner when men went to pay the tithe, and a train trip to Shrewsbury Flower Show for the church choir (men and boys).

For Harvest Festival farmers provide oats, wheat and barley for ladies to make plaited wreaths to decorate the church pillars, pulpit, lectern, font and porch. They are sent the next week to decorate another church.

Comberford ☙

The village of Comberford lies approximately one mile west of Wigginton which is approximately 1½ miles north of Tamworth. The two villages share the same parish priest.

The village consists mainly of the manor house, now known as Comberford Hall, which is converted into luxury flats. The adjoining coach-house and out-buildings have been converted into dwellings, and the village is approached via a gated lodge. There is a manor farm, several old cottages and new houses, and the villagers worship at the church of St Mary and St George.

The Comberford family boasted ancient lineage. Henry I, son of William the Conqueror, bequeathed the manor of Comberford, which included much of the land around Wigginton, to Alano, for services rendered during the Norman Conquest, and he took the title of the village – Alano de Comberford.

Loyalty to the Crown enriched them over the centuries and by 1391 John de Comberford possessed property in Tamworth. When Tamworth church was destroyed by fire the Comberford family paid for the restoration of St Katherine's chapel in the north transept and it became known as the Comberford chapel.

In the 1640s, when Cromwell marched on Tamworth, the church was stripped of its statues, and the tombs were desecrated. Colonel William Comberford was High Steward of Stafford and had given £1000 to the

Royal cause and garrisoned the towns of Tamworth and Stafford against the Parliamentarians, but to no avail. Charles I was beheaded and William was stripped of his property. Later his nephew, Robert inherited Comberford Manor.

In 1656 the manor house and contents were valued at £160! The unfortunate Comberford family never recovered their wealth, and those who survived followed the Stuarts into exile in France, and never returned.

Coppenhall ҉

Coppenhall is a parish and a village three miles south-west of Stafford and 4 miles north-west from Penkridge railway station. In the Domesday Book of 1086 the village was called 'Copehale' and by the 12th century it had become known as 'Coppenhale' which means 'The Meadow Land of Coppa'.

There was a church in Coppenhall in 1200 and it subsequently became a dependency of Penkridge College. In 1563 it was described as a chapel of ease to Penkridge. The church of St Lawrence is a small stone building consisting of a nave and chancel with a timber bell turret at the west end, and is of special interest as a comparatively unaltered example of a small church of the year 1200. The churchyard was not consecrated for burials until 1870. Since 1892 it has been united with the church of St Leonard, Dunston.

In 1700 Coppenhall House was lived in by Parker Williams. He was the village wheelwright and worked on the nearby farms in the village. By the early 1800s the house was owned by a country gentleman, Edward Augustus Bartlam, who owned much land in and around the village. The villagers through the centuries have been very superstitious and the haunting of Coppenhall House was well known. It was thought to have a haunted four poster bed, which was sold at auction in 1981.

The farming families in the village today are descendants of those living here in 1700. The Holt family still owns Hall Farm and the Madders are a prominent farming family in the village. Coppenhall Farm changed its name to Church Farm in the 18th century and is made up of a large proportion of land in the village today.

Butterhill Mill at Coppenhall

From the wardens' post, during the Second World War, the city of Liverpool, 70 miles away, and the city of Coventry 40 miles away could be seen on fire as the German bombers attacked them. When the bombers flew over Stafford to attack English Electric, Coppenhall was in the flight path. Only one bomb fell on English Electric and fortunately that failed to explode. Coppenhall House on the other hand came under attack in the Civil War of 1640 and was hit by a cannonball!

There were two mills in Coppenhall. One may have stood in The Windmill Field in Chaseview Lane, while the second stood on high ground some 150 yards west of Butterhill Farm and was said locally to be the only six sail mill in the county in use by 1820.

The main roads through the village are now wide enough for two cars to pass, just about; but this is only since 1950 when more houses in the village were constructed. Chase View House and Coppenhall House have gradually sold off land to the developers as building plots, but Coppenhall remains a small, peaceful village, despite its many changes in the last century.

Coven

Coven was originally a manor in the parish of Brewood. It is situated 2 miles south east of Brewood and on the western fringe of the Black Country. It is recorded that Coven was held by Ailric before the Conquest and by Robert Stafford in 1086. In 1166 it gave its name to the family of Alan de Coven, who held a knights fee under Robert Stafford. Such manorial rights as still existed in 1956 were held by Major R F Monkton.

Throughout the 1800s Coven was known as a working village, with locksmiths, chain-making and iron smelting. On Brewood Road there is a William and Mary cottage dated 1679, which was the home for priests from Brewood, and in the 1930s was a police station. The village also housed two bakeries, blacksmiths and a wheelwright. Bricks were hand made at Light Ash and a water mill stood at Standeford. One mill in Coven village was burnt down giving rise to the name Burnt Mill and nearby is Jacksons Bridge, so called after a man named Jackson who hanged himself beneath the bridge.

Mr John Smith, who was a local preacher, gave part of his garden in Lawn Lane for the building of a Methodist church in 1839. To get to the chapel the minister had to pass through Mr Smiths' cottage. In 1857 St Paul's Anglican church was built on land given by Mr George Monkton. The stones were provided by Mr Thomas Giffard, the descendant of whom lives in Chillington Manor in the grounds of which it is said a panther was once killed by a bow and arrow! The old school in School Lane was used by the Church before St Paul's was built and was known as a chapel of ease.

In Coven there are seven mobile home sites situated in various parts of the village. The first recorded population of the village was in 1851 when there were 800 but the population in 1987 was 3,281, showing how the village has grown during that time with shops, local inns and a country club.

Coven is now very modern with new houses, bungalows, shops and businesses, but there are still several of the old houses, such as Grange Farm where once King Charles stayed, on his way to Moseley Old Hall. Opposite the modern shops stands the old Poplar Farm Cottage and where the Croft Garage stands was once a poultry farm. The village is flanked by the Staffordshire and Worcestershire canals and the river Penk runs through the village.

Denstone 🦢

Around Denstone in the Churnet valley the land rises sharply. The Weaver Hills seem to change with the weather; sometimes they look near and green, sometimes blue and far away. Seen from the top of College Hill the village is spectacularly beautiful, especially in May when the damson trees are in blossom. Denstone damsons are the very best. Thousands of strikes of the fruit have been bought for city markets and many more are sent to Lancashire for use in dyes for the textile industry. What a superb colour!

For hundreds of years the village was divided into Denstone-in-Rocester and Denstone-in-Alton (or Alverton). Not until the late 19th century did it become a separate parish. But individual histories date from earlier times. The brothers Bott, who lived in Stubwood until the

1960s, were descendants of the John Bott who was taxed three shillings for his land in 1327!

Denstone Hall is built on the site of an ancient seat of the Okeover family and was the scene of a murder in 1293. Ancient timbers remain in the present house and a mud and wattle wall, although it was re-fronted and partly rebuilt in 1853. That was the year that it was occupied by Mr Boden, great grandfather of the present owner.

For 200 years successive generations of the Walker family were licensees of the Tavern, dated 1669, which is one of a number of 17th and 18th century buildings within easy reach of the centre of the village.

Denstone's greatest benefactor was Sir Thomas Percival Heywood of Doveleys. Between 1860 and 1880 he built the exquisite All Saints' church, the school, the vicarage and Denstone College. Thanks to him the village now had a separate identity and a focus for its social and religious life.

This is a vigorous community with a strong local feeling. No fewer than six Best Kept Village awards are the evidence of pride and hard effort. The village school is a focal point for the community. The village post office is basic to its needs. Tennis and Bowls Clubs flourish, as they have for many years on the British Legion Sports Ground. On Armistice Sunday a large crowd gathers at the war memorial. The annual Variety Show is composed entirely of home grown entertainment, and a Sports Trust aims to provide continuing facilities for all.

Derrington

Derrington village lies three miles west of Stafford amid rural surroundings, nestling in the shadow of historic Stafford castle on the hill on one side and ancient Bury Ring on the other. More recently progress has intruded on this peaceful village with the advent of the M6 motorway, which passes between Derrington and the County Town.

In the Domesday Book, Derrington was known as Dodintone. In 1900 it consisted of 5 farms and 20–25 cottages compared with about 300 dwellings today (mostly built post-war) and one working farm.

St Matthew's church was built of sand-stone in the Early English style in 1847, and endowed at the sole personal expense of the Rev Charles

Smith-Royds, MA, rector of Haughton. It was designed by Henry Ward, architect of Stafford, who also designed the Borough Hall. Over the years there have been many donations in memory of loved ones, enriching the interior of the church, and time lovingly given by devoted villagers in countless different ways.

After 7 years of hard work by voluntary workers, the village hall was completed in 1935 and later extended to include a thriving village Club. The hall is the centre for most of the varied village activities. Derrington also has its own football team.

Years ago, Derrington had four shops, the only remaining one being The Village Stores, once the front room of a cottage, but now much extended and modernised. The Post Office opened in 1932 and is still run by the same family today.

The Red Lion public house opened in the early 19th century and has been extended to include a restaurant. In the past when there was no running water in the village, the villagers collected their water from the village pump outside the Red Lion. .

In the 1800's Derrington had a cobbler, reputed to have made shoes for the Royal family. There was also a Blacksmith who owned the Forge and the Three Horseshoes Public House (now gone)! As they were next door to each other, this enabled the farmers to have a drink while waiting for their horses to be shod.

Old Hall Cottage was built in 1606 and the Old Hall about 1708, with thatched roof, walls of wattle and daub and old ship's timbers. A well-worn stone covers a deep well in the garden bearing the initials 'S.D.' and 1606. The date of 1612 appears above the doorway of Blue Cross Farm, and the Bowyer family who lived at Stallbrook Hall, were given manorial rights by Henry VIII in 1552.

Doxey 🌿

To those who merely pass through it on their way from Stafford to the West, or to Newport and the Shropshire border, Doxey may seem indistinguishable from the rest of Stafford. But less than 100 years ago, the small hamlet of Doxey, with fewer than 20 houses, was well outside the town area and an integral part of the parish of Seighford where much of it remains as far as civil parish boundaries are concerned. For most of the people who have lived here for some time, and this includes a surprisingly large percentage of the population, and who have seen it grow rapidly over the last 50 years, Doxey retains its village atmosphere.

An Ordnance Survey map of 1881 shows less than 10 houses in the area of Doxey, some of which can be readily identified today. The black and white house next to the modern church is very old, as is Doxey House, a 17th century listed building, now carefully restored by the Borough Council and providing some of the accommodation for the very new old people's flats. Other buildings still in use are Brookhouse Farm and what used to be smaller cottages nearby, and the two cottages on the Stafford side of the new church.

And what of Doxey today? It has grown from the tiny hamlet of the last century when most of the very few inhabitants were concerned with agriculture or were 'in service' at larger houses, until today there are approximately 1500 adult electors in Doxey following a large variety of occupations both in the area and further afield. Some are employed in the timber yard of Henry Venables which has grown from the sawmills established in 1864 to its present large business, where craftsmen do intricate highly-skilled work for places like York Minister. On the other hand, the railways, once a major employer, need less people now, and one of the main lines is now sadly disused, following cuts made many years ago, though, as it is now owned by the County Council, it does still provide a walkway for local people.

Draycott in the Moors ༄

Before the coming of the Romans, Draycott in the Moors was one of several British settlements. In Roman times it was a legionary outpost, the rock face at the back of the post office has shelving and other features suggesting it was used in shoeing horses or repairing chariots.

In Georgian and Victorian eras Draycott was a popular place for the sport of cock fighting and the cock ring can still be clearly seen today. The parish church is called St Margaret's and on or near St Margaret's Day, 20th July, would be held Draycott Wake when cock fighting was a part of the celebrations.

The Rev William Draycott, priest from 1502–1512 instituted the Draycott dole, distributed in Mid Lent each year to the poor, the amount of the dole £1 6s 8d given in bread and herrings every Sunday in Lent, and anything over in pork on Easter Eve. Nowadays money is given just during Mid Lent. Also until quite recently Mid Lent Sunday was called Fig-Pie or Figgy-Pudding Sunday – the pies were delicious.

After the Reformation the Catholic community moved to a chapel at nearby Paynsley Hall, where the Draycotts, Lords of the Manor, had lived since 1496. In 1791 a small Catholic church called St Mary's was built at Cresswell in the parish of Draycott.

Draycott could never be classed 'Olde Worlde' because a main road runs through the centre and hence there is no village green. However, there is just a small part off the main road which still retains a little of yesteryear, a stream and ducks and a lovely old house, where the owner takes tremendous pride in the garden.

About a mile and a half away from Draycott is a spot called Slade Mans Hole, where during a battle, soldiers were slain, and legend has it that if something was thrown up into the nearby rocks a soldier would appear. Many years ago a young girl, having been to Tean to collect medicine for her grandmother who lived in Draycott, decided to throw a stone to see what would happen. This she did only to take fright and run when she heard a noise. Not until arriving at Grandmother's did she realise the noise had been the cork coming off the medicine bottle!

Drayton Bassett ⍟

Drayton Bassett is to be found in the extreme south-east corner of Staffordshire, bordering Warwickshire. After the Conquest William kept Drayton and the surrounding valuable parkland for himself but it later came to the Bassett family. In the 13th century the Bassetts built a manor house and enclosed surrounding parkland. They also built a church, of which remains only part of the tower base, on possibly the site of an earlier church.

Later the Bassetts appear to have moved their manor house to a more wooded area of the park, on a slight incline, overlooking the village. It was this estate, nearby mills, and a plentiful water supply to power machinery that attracted Robert Peel in the 1790s. He was the third son of Robert 'Parsley' Peel, the northern cotton industrialist.

His son, the future Sir Robert Peel – the great Prime Minister and founder of the police force was brought up at Drayton. He chose burial here in his own church rather than the honour of Westminster Abbey. He had much of his father's house rebuilt and extended to house his art collection. It became a splendid mansion where the most important people of his day were entertained. In November 1843 it had its most famous visitor – Queen Victoria, accompanied by Prince Albert.

Robert Peel senior, his famous son and other Peels carried out building programmes in the village also. Indeed their hand is still seen today. Several cottages near the green have no front doors, their only entrances are at the rear. Popular stories tell that the second Sir Robert either disliked being stared at or that he disapproved of villagers standing at their front doors gossiping. His wife, Lady Julia, established a school in the village in 1830; the building is now the village post office and shop. Another popular story tells that she was responsible for Drayton being publess. The large house facing the green was once the public house The White Lion and presumably villagers would have gathered there to gossip! It is said that Sir Robert had the licence withdrawn so that Lady Peel would not be offended by such a sight when she drove to church on a Sunday in her carriage. The pub became a post office and you can still see the post box mark in the wall. At the turn of this century the fourth Sir Robert built the long row of houses known as New Row or Swiss Cottages. They were built in a decorative Swiss style with all the modern conveniences of the day.

The Peel family fortunes declined and what was left of the estate and the manor house was put up for sale in 1926. What became of the house is not quite clear. All that remains is the old clock tower to the stables and some out-buildings. The name of the last Peel is to be found on the war memorial in the churchyard.

In Drayton Bassett's history its position has always been of the utmost importance. After the 'great' period of the Peels it might well have become a backwater but for its nearness to the city of Birmingham. The Foseco factory was built on part of Drayton Manor in 1952 mainly because of closeness to Birmingham. Today excellent access to major roads has made Drayton a very desirable place to live for those who commute to Birmingham and other Midland towns and cities. Drayton

Manor Park and Zoo is visited by many thousands of people a year, who find it a pleasant break from city life.

Eccleshall ✒️

Eccleshall's name derives from its religious importance – church by a hollow – and for many centuries the bishops of Lichfield resided at Eccleshall Castle; indeed six bishops lie buried in, or near, the church. Today religion is still very much alive, with growing co-operation between Anglicans, Methodists and Roman Catholics, drawing the inhabitants closer together spiritually as well as socially.

Being in the centre of a wide farming area the village brought the farming community together for its weekly sale of livestock and produce. It was a disappointment to many when the cattle market closed in recent years. The fact that Eccleshall was also on the main mail-coach route from London to Chester increased its importance as a staging post on this arduous journey and seemed to create the need for an excessive number of hostelries! The streets are still graced by a variety of old coaching inns, each with its own character and appeal. The charm of the High Street lies in these and other old buildings – some elegant houses, others converted to shops, banks, offices – all now protected by a conservation order and providing an attractive shopping venue for residents and visitors alike.

About seven miles to the north-west of Eccleshall, near the border with Shropshire, the river Sow rises and meanders through peaceful country-side to the county town of Stafford. A little over a mile from Eccleshall the river flows through the lovely Ice Age lake, Copmere, lying amongst attractive scattered hamlets. Forty five acres in extent and fringed by reeds and woodland, Copmere forms the centre of a series of nature reserves owned or leased by dedicated people wishing to conserve the natural beauty of this quiet rural area. Both river and lake are beloved by fishermen and naturalists, and Copmere is easily accessible by the hand-icapped, for it is bordered by two minor roads and a public footpath.

A ladies' folk dance group performing in Eccleshall High Street   71

Edingale

The village of Edingale lies beside the river Mease about 6 miles from Tamworth and 8 miles from Lichfield. It has a population of about 350 many of whom commute to work in neighbouring towns. It has a church, a school, a village shop/post office and one public house. Expansion of the village is limited by agricultural land and near the river by the threat of flooding.

At one time the centre of the village was at Croxall not Edingale, though the settlement there has almost disappeared, only the church and Hall remaining since Edingale became the centre of population. It is believed that one of the church bells (dated 1685) was moved from Croxall.

Holy Trinity church was built in 1881, the former building having been struck by lightning and destroyed by fire. That church was apparently of little architectural interest though the small Saxon window incorporated in the present building leads to the belief that there has been a place of worship there for ten centuries. There are church records dating back to 1575. Church Farm and cottages in Schofield Lane dating from the 17th century are still occupied.

Census records available from the middle of the last century show the names of farms – Raddle, Pessall, Edingale Fields etc, which are still occupied and farmed today and families with the same names as found in these records (Rowley, Collingwood, Dicken, Wilcox) are still living in the village.

Undoubtedly Edingale has had well-known residents in the past but of recent years the best known was Mr Holland of Edingale House Farm – 'Jos' as he was known. He lived there from 1909 until his death in 1986 at the age of 96. He was known all over the country as a breeder and judge of Shire horses. He bred many champions in his time, probably the most famous being *Edingale Mascot* now at stud in the United States spreading the name of Edingale beyond the boundaries of Staffordshire.

Ellastone 🌿

Ellastone is separated from Derbyshire by the river Dove. It covers an area of 1417 acres and the 1985 records show that it has a population of 240. The land at Ellastone was once owned by the Earls of Shrewsbury, then by the Bromley Davenports and latterly by both the Silcock estate and the Bamford family.

The parish church of St Peter was built on an old foundation of around the 12th century and the present building is around 300 years old. The only original parts remaining are the north chancel which is dated 1588 and the tower which has an inscription plate dated 1586, while the nave externally was reconstructed in 1830. The monuments of the occupants of Calwich Abbey are in the church but the earliest effigies, which are of Sir Richard Fleetwood and his wife, are badly damaged and defaced.

The remaining three pinnacles of the west tower of St Peter's were demolished because one pinnacle fell down in a gale in January 1976. The parishioners have a tremendous task in trying to raise over £70,000 for a new roof and other repairs if the church is to remain open.

The most influential house in Ellastone used to be Calwich Abbey, situated between Ellastone and Mayfield on the banks of the river Dove, founded about 1149. The original house on the site of the monastery was pulled down in the 18th century and rebuilt just above the stream: a long white house with bow windows approached by an avenue across the park. In 1927 this great estate was sold off in lots and the house demolished. Little survives to remind us of the former grandeur of Calwich Abbey except the fishing temple at the end of the lake bearing the date, 1797.

A cottage which attracts much attention in the village is called Adam Bede because of its connection with the Evans family and with Mary Ann Evans, alias George Eliot, the novelist. It is suggested that Ellastone is the 'Hayslope' of her novel *Adam Bede* and that one of the brothers who lived in the cottage was used for her characterisation of Adam Bede. A case can also be made that Mount Pleasant was the model for 'Poyser's Cottage' and Goodall's Farm is the 'Hall Farm' in her novel.

Ellastone Old Hall can be found on the main Uttoxeter to Ashbourne road which runs through the village. It is a fine example of a late 17th century building having 5 bays and a doorway with pilasters. The Hall was later used as one of the two village pubs and called the Bromley

Arms after the famous family in the village but today it is functioning as an antiques shop.

At one time farming was the main occupation along with service in the big houses in the area and with road mending and repairing. The village of Ellastone no longer relies on these three industries to provide employment but parishioners work in the nearby towns or have to leave and find employment further afield.

With the church in decline and the village school closed, the community around Ellastone now congregate for meetings, dances and festivities of all kinds at the village hall, opened in August 1911. It was designed and built by Sir Percival Heywood of Wootton Lodge and all monies needed for it were subscribed in one night at a meeting in the village.

Endon ✿

Endon lies in a green and well-watered valley in north-west Staffordshire. The name derives from the Anglo-Saxon Heandun, meaning 'high hill' or 'hill fort', corrupted in the Domesday Book to Enendun.

On the hilltop today stands the square-towered parish church of St Luke, erected in 1730 as a chapel of ease. Inside are beautiful stained glass windows, including an east window by Burne-Jones, and outside a panoramic view of the surrounding countryside.

Below in the oldest part of Endon, known as 'the village', are weathered stone cottages, some converted from early 18th century weaving sheds; one was the former Black Horse Inn and two others the old smithy and the village shop. Two modest brick cottages bear the inscription 'Wesleyan Chapel, erected 1835', replaced by a handsome chapel built half-a-mile away in 1876. In Brook Lane the stream is crossed by a ford and an attractive stone footbridge was added in 1981.

Several impressive stone farmhouses are situated on the village outskirts, the oldest dating from 1561, with evidence of earlier monastic use provided by monks' cells in the vaulted cellar and a medieval fishpond. On the main road, the painted sign on the bow-windowed Plough Inn covers a whole wall and at the 'new' Black Horse a short distance away, sandbags were always kept ready in wet weather, to stem incoming water from the over-flowing Endon Brook. Work on the watercourse since 1983 has improved the situation.

By-passed many years ago by the A53, the village is a picturesque conservation area, enlivened by the Well Dressing Festivities held annually at Spring Bank Holiday. The stone well, fed by an unfailing spring, was given in 1845 by Thomas Heaton, a local landowner.

Winding past Endon at some 490 feet above sea level, the Caldon canal, built by James Brindley in 1777, is believed to be the highest in England. Disused commercially, restoration by the Caldon Canal Society and British Waterways has brought designation as a Leisure Cruiseway.

The railway, opened in 1870, not now carrying passengers but still used to convey limestone from Cauldon Lowe quarries, brought improved accessibility which encouraged the building of some imposing Victorian villas. Most development has taken place since the mid 1950s with the building of a housing estate swelling the population from about 2,000 in 1949 to around 3,800.

In the past local employment was partly provided by a potters mill and a stone quarry but present-day villagers work mainly in Stoke-on-Trent and Leek. Farming continues in the locality: there is an old-established corn merchant, an agricultural haulier and a working forge. The late Charles Perkin, father of the present blacksmith, was champion of England in his trade and his son's skill produced the 'Endon' sign placed at the northern main road boundary. Social activities centre round the refurbished village hall.

Etching Hill

Etching Hill village lies one mile to the north-west of Rugeley at the edge of Cannock Chase. The main feature of Etching Hill is the hill itself which rises steeply to 454 feet above sea level and 100 feet above the houses of the village. The hill is capped with an outcrop of red sandstone and its lower slopes are covered with gorse, bracken and heather. On a clear day in the distance can be seen the hills of Shropshire, the Derbyshire Peak District and just a mile or two away, the local landmarks of Stile Cop and Castle Ring. The rivers Trent and Blythe meander through the meadow lands and behind the town of Rugeley the giant cooling towers of the power station dominate the skyline.

In the early 1800s the village consisted mainly of a few cottages built in the lee of the hill sheltering from the prevailing winds. As the town of Rugeley prospered local businessmen and tradespeople built large houses around the hill and moved out of town to live nearer to the Chase. During the late 1960s and early 1970s a major building project took place, with hundreds of homes being built on the green fields to the north and east of the hill linking Etching Hill to Rugeley.

In 1880 a generous local landowner gave an area of land to the south-west of the hill and part of the hill itself to local inhabitants and it is administered under a charitable trust. Part of the land was to be made into allotments for the 'benefit of the labouring poor' and the other part, including the hill, was to be made available for the 'benefit of the inhabitants of the ancient parish of Rugeley' and so is safe from future development.

At the foot of the hill stands the church of the Holy Spirit. It is of modern design and on Whit Sunday 17th May 1964, five months after the foundation stone had been laid, the new church was dedicated by the Bishop of Lichfield. The church replaced a small corrugated iron and timber Mission Room that was erected in 1882 by the villagers.

The hill itself has been the scene of many important events over the years. Local residents stood on the summit during the Second World War and saw the sky lit with a fiery glow as German bombs were dropped on the Black Country. On a happier note torchlight processions have left Rugeley and wound their way to the top of the hill and bonfires have been lit to celebrate the Armistice ending the First World War, the Jubilee of King George V and the Coronation of King George VI.

The village of Etching Hill borders on green belt land adjoining Cannock Chase which is designated an Area of Outstanding Natural Beauty.

Flash 🦌

Flash is in the parish of Quarnford and claims to be the highest village in England at 1,518 feet above sea level and the most northerly point of Staffordshire. There is a church, school, inn, village hall, post office and shop. The church was erected in 1744 and rebuilt in 1901.

The village hall was opened in 1958 by Mrs Jessie Evans from the Staffordshire Rural Community Council. It was built as a memorial to men killed in the Second World War, by village people helped by the Quakers and students from all over the world. Electricity came to the village in 1962 and mains water in March 1984. There has not been any building done in or around the village since the 1950s.

The building which used to be the school house is now the post office and shop. It is open every day from 10 am to 6 pm and adjoins the New Inn. A man named Tom Wardle used to live at the New Inn in the 1800s, who was a clog maker.

The Flash Loyal Union Society was established on 27th July 1846. This is a club into which people pay an annual subscription as insurance against them being sick and unable to work. The local name for the Society is the 'Teapot Club' because it was said they kept the money in a tea pot. There is an annual 'Club Feast'. It used to be on the third Monday in June, now it is on the Saturday nearest the third Monday.

There used to be a cattle market in the village on the last Friday in every month and Flash Fair on 29th September when people could also sell sheep and other things.

A lady called Charlotte (Lottie) Slack died in 1987 at the age of 99 who, with Sarah Brocklehurst and other women, used to make buttons for a mill in Leek. They would have to walk to Leek to fetch their materials and return the buttons – about 8 miles each way.

There is a legend which says counterfeit money was made at Flash, ie 'Flash Money', at a cottage known as Wolfe Edge. The pedlars believed that if they took their wares away by way of the Three Shires Head and the law came after them, they could be out of Staffordshire and into Derbyshire or into Cheshire all within seconds as at this point all three counties meet, so unless all counties had police at that place they would easily resist arrest.

Foxt

Foxt is a pleasant little village, 4 miles north of Cheadle, just off the A52 Stoke-on-Trent to Ashbourne road. It is set along a straggling narrow road which rises steeply from the floor of the Churnet valley at Froghall, upwards to the top of a ridge two miles away. This rise is some 800 feet in all, and consists of a series of steep banks, sharp bends with some level stretches.

Along this road there are over 100 houses, a shop, a public house, a village hall, a church and even an odd patch or two of common land. The houses are scattered along the road from the Truck Hole at Froghall right up to the top of the Casey, which is a very old road, or 'Causeway'.

The houses standing today have been built in a variety of styles and materials, as they have changed over the years. The oldest houses were built in the 17th century. Foxt Town is a group of farms built, perhaps as a grange to Croxden Abbey, with their land as a sort of strip system further up the road. Since that time other houses have appeared as land has been cleared, and as various tradesmen have set up their businesses.

The ironstone boom of the latter half of the 19th century has left few signs of the tramways and engine houses that went with it. There are, however, a number of spoil heaps in the Foxtwood area, which serve as a reminder of the coal workings, although these are now grassed over.

The biggest single housing project occurred in 1911, when Messrs Thomas Bolton & Sons built 24 houses at the lower end of the village. These were to accommodate skilled workers from their Birmingham factory, which they were closing and transferring to their premises at Froghall. They also laid the foundations for a further 16 houses, but these were never built.

Foxt church was built in 1839 in an uncompromising square style with a tower. It is a small enough to be intimate though it has none of the theatrical beauty of older churches with their pillars, arches and old memorials. For some obscure reason, the church was not consecrated until 1899, and was used firstly by the Methodists before they built their own chapel in 1859, and shortly by the school before Foxt school was built by public subscription in 1877. The school closed in 1984 due to a shortage of children, and has since been used as a village hall.

The Fox & Goose is the last remaining pub in the village. It has been modernised and extended, whilst its malthouse has recently been converted into a house. The bulk of Foxt people commute to their work outside the village, though it is no longer the copper works at Froghall nor the quarries at Caldon Low that provide the majority with employment.

Fradley 🐚

Fradley is part of the parish of Alrewas and in the 12th century was called Frodeleye. It is situated just off the A38 – the old Ryknild Way that was built by the Romans. Until recently the village consisted of St Stephen's church, the school, a number of farms and small-holdings and a few private dwellings. Today the village has altered dramatically.

The church of St Stephen stands proud. It was consecrated on 23rd May 1861 and was built thanks to the then vicar of Alrewas, the Rev Hazelhurst, who felt that it was too far to carry the dead to Alrewas for burial. The church school was built in 1874 and along with the church was built of bricks carried by locals from the then brickyard at Hilliards Cross where they were made. The school is now used as a Youth Centre and a bigger school has been built.

A great number of the farms have vanished along with the small-holdings leaving only the Old Hall, Bycars Farm, Bridge Farm and Hilliards Cross. The Old Hall goes back a number of centuries and a coat of arms used to adorn the front of the building. At one time a moat used to surround the house but this was filled in when the then occupiers' two daughters both died of scarlet fever which was thought to have been caused by an infection caught from the stagnant water in the moat. Hilliards Cross was originally a shooting lodge and was known as Eaglestone House: so called whan an eagle was seen to land on the chimney during its building. Since becoming a farm Hilliards Cross has remained in the same family.

In 1920 point-to-point races were held on Fradley common, but this was taken over by the RAF in 1939 and an airfield was constructed. Hurricanes were despatched to squadrons engaged in the Battle of Britain, in 1941 came the Spitfire and then the airfield came under the control of No. 6 Group Bomber Command and with this came the famous Wellington Bomber. The RAF finally left in 1957 and most of the land was put back to agriculture and the housing taken over by the Lichfield District Council.

All the small-holdings have disappeared but one building remains the same in appearance at least. The Old Smithy, where farmers used to bring their horses to be shod stands at the entrance to the village. Close to this stands the oldest listed building in Fradley. Originally two cottages with a cruck beam, it is now used as a workshop. From here an agricultural contractor carried out his business of threshing corn, travelling from farm to farm with his machinery which was driven by steam. The two original steam engines are now in Lincolnshire, still both working.

New houses keep appearing all around and the next few years will see the opening of an industrial estate on part of the old airfield. One of the first events will be the opening of a new livestock market and fine arts sale rooms.

Canals surround Fradley and a local beauty spot, Fradley Junction, is where the Trent and Mersey canal meet the Coventry canal.

Fulford 🦚

The village of Fulford lies approximately 3 miles south of the old Roman Road as it passes through Draycott and Blythe Bridge. It is off the beaten track and approached by narrow country lanes. The hamlets of Crossgate, Mossgate and Spotgate lie near to it.

The history of Fulford is buried very deeply. Its beginnings go back to Anglo Saxon times as one of the possessions of the Royal House of Mercia and was mentioned in the Domesday Book as 'Foleford'. In the 12th century Fulford Manor seems to have been appropriated to the priory of Augustinian Canons. At the Dissolution of the Monasteries Fulford was divided into fair sized farms, and cattle were seized during the Civil War by the Roundheads because the inhabitants refused to contribute to their cause.

In the 18th century Fulford came into the hands of the family of Allen, one of whom became Dean of Chester and for some time the Lords of the Manor came from the descendants of that family.

Fulford remained a sleepy village until recent times, with its church, school (now replaced, but founded in 1785 and standing on the village green by the village pump) and Public House (the Shoulder of Mutton). Now the sleepy remains can still be seen but there has been considerable modern development. The village still only boasts one shop-cum-Post Office and is still relatively isolated.

The church lies away from the new development and is the only one in the Archdeanery of Stoke-on-Trent to be dedicated to St Nicholas. The old yews in the churchyard seem to point to it being a very early place of worship, and certainly a church has been there since the 14th century. In the early 19th century the church seems to have been the 'Gretna Green' of North Staffordshire with many runaway couples from the Longton District being married there. The present church was erected in 1825 and resorted in 1897.

Stallington Hall, one mile from Fulford church was owned by the Child family until early this century when it was sold by Sir Hill-Child. Their special pew can be seen at the rear of the church. The Hall now belongs to the City of Stoke-on-Trent and is used as a home for the mentally ill.

Glascote ﷼

At the beginning of the 19th century Glascote was a pretty, happy little village, where a few hundred people lived, mostly farmworkers and their families.

By 1854 the hamlet had grown, a good thick seam of clay had been discovered under the green fields, coal was found, and people started to move in. The people managed to build themselves a small church and row upon row of cottages and terraced houses were hastily constructed. Within 30 years the population had swollen to 3,000.

As more houses and small shops appeared on street corners, the population grew too large for the small church so a new church was built in two years, in Bamford Street, and inaugurated on 30th April 1880. The small church was then used as a school.

It was at St George's church, before the altar, that the new vicar of Tamworth prayed in 1914 for the men going to war. His name was Maurice Berkley Peel, a grandson of the great Sir Robert. He went to France as chaplain to the Forces, was awarded the Military Cross in 1915 but returned home severely wounded. In 1917 he volunteered to return to the trenches knowing the needs of the men. In May of that year whilst out searching for the wounded, he was shot dead by a German sniper. A year later, Glascote church paid tribute to this 'modern day saint'. A statue of St George was erected outside the church in memory of Maurice Peel, and there it stands today.

Two chapels were also built, the Methodist and Primitive Methodist, a

Working Men's Club, the Dolphin Inn and the Anchor Inn by the canal. After the Second World War the industries of Glascote began to disappear and the coal mine closed. Most of the old shops have gone now, a few still remain but now are used for different purposes and owned by different people. The boys school which was later called the Glascote MacGregor Boys School is still there. Now gone are the smells of new made bread, the sound of the anvil, and the smell of tar and paint from the boat yards, the chink of harness and the clip clop of the old Shire horses on their way to the stables after a hard days work pulling the coal barges, the whirl of the sawmills and the smell of sawdust. The old railway and loco have all gone now – to make way for large housing estates.

Gnosall 🌿

The village of Gnosall was mentioned in the Domesday Book under its ancient title of Geneshall and this name has been perpetuated in modern street names.

The oldest building is the church of St Lawrence, parts of which date from 1080. It was one of the five Chapels Royal of Mercia. Nearby, now in the process of restoration, is the Duke's Head which has an Elizabethan facade but a much older central structure.

The old lock-up which was in danger of demolition to make way for road widening was saved from destruction by the efforts of the WI who raised funds to move it to its present site at the side of the A518 overlooking the village. It is said that the custodian, the sole keyholder, rode out from Stafford to bring victuals or release to the unfortunate prisoner who would have been in great danger if the custodian failed to arrive as a result of bad weather. The windowless prison would not allow any relatives to provide any sustenance to the wrongdoer imprisoned in its cold stone walls.

The coming of the canal and the railway changed Gnosall from a hamlet into a much larger village. Alongside the canal was a cement works producing Roman cement, prior to Portland cement, which was used in the construction of the Manchester Ship Canal and Liverpool Docks because of its waterproof characteristics. Adjacent to this was a brickworks and further along the canal a mill said to have marketed the first self-raising flour in this country. The cement works and the brickworks competed with one another, not for business, but for the greatest number of employees! The canal is still well used today principally for pleasure and the tow paths provide pleasant walking. Sadly the last passenger train ran in 1964 and since then the railway bridge which formed a landmark in the village has been removed although the booking office has been preserved in a Staffordshire museum. The railway line, devoid of its track, now forms a leisure walk to a local beauty spot called Broadhill where an old windmill has been incorporated in a modern house.

The educational needs of the village have been well served over the centuries by a free grammar school and a Dame school. With the advent of the first Education Act, a school was built which forms part of the present St Lawrence First School campus.

Today the residents have a wealth of clubs and societies which help to conserve the character and the amenities of the village. Internationally famous are Gnosall Handbell Ringers, who have kept alive an ancient tradition in the village and have appeared on TV and radio. Their future should be assured because 119 bells are now in trust for the village.

Great Haywood, Little Haywood & Colwich ✍

Whilst Domesday's 'Haywood Magna' was the busiest and most important, today these three villages in one, share the same Parish Council and theoretical 'rights' and 'privileges' on Cannock Chase. Situated 7 miles south of Stafford they straddle the old direct route from London to the North West, via Chester. The river Trent and Trent and Mersey canal run through the villages, and Great Haywood boasts a canal junction and wharf – now serving pleasure, not working, narrow-boats.

From the early 1960s onwards, new housing estates have replaced Georgian, Victorian and more ancient properties, although still extant are fine examples of these, some going back to medieval times. Victorian survivals include Railway Cottages, those in Colwich built by the London & North-Western, and Little Haywood's by the North Staffs ('Notty') companies. Prior to the Industrial Revolution estate cottages in Trent Lane, with Shugborough Terrace and Anson Row housed 'cottage industries' – as also that unique circle 'The Ring'. Whilst the first three stand, modernised internally, the original Ring (comprising 14 cottages, with bakehouse, wash-house and well in the centre) was destroyed – replaced by bungalows!

Village industries in the past included brewing – hence Brewery Lane leading to Brewery Yard – and all the usual country and village trades, whilst the tall chimney of Colwich Brickworks still stands. The derelict site is now a conservation area – although in the early 1980s only the intervention of the Water Authority's geologists averted the construction of a County rubbish tip! Today the village produces agricultural implements, has a corn-mill, and a leisure industry comprising two pleasure-boat companies, garden-centres, four pubs (The Clifford Arms on the site of a coaching-inn) and the usual clutch of village societies and activities.

There are three schools – Colwich's having been founded in 1828 by the aristocratic Miss Charlotte Sparrow of Bishton Hall, still honoured on her birthday by schoolchildren's posies on her grave – and four churches. St Michael's Colwich is on the site of St Chad's chapel-in-the-woods, Great Haywood's St Stephen's church was originally a chapel-of-ease to Colwich, St John's Roman Catholic church was in 1845 dismantled stone by stone and moved from Tixall by locals of the faith to be re-erected in Great Haywood, 2 miles away, and there is a chapel, recently re-opened. There is an abbey in Colwich (once a hunting lodge for the Earls of Shrewsbury) sheltering an enclosed order of nuns, and a house in Great Haywood of vast antiquity known as The Abbey, though curiously, never used for this purpose.

The Essex Bridge over the confluence of the Sow with the Trent, leading from Great Haywood to Shugborough was, originally, a wooden structure, later replaced by a fourteen-arched stone packhorse bridge – the longest in England. Legend has it that the Earl of Essex was instrumental in its construction for his Queen, Elizabeth I, to make her way to the Chase, for hunting! There is also a cast-metal bridge over the waterways – now only over the canal. Weetman's Bridge in Little Haywood is reputedly haunted by a weeping woman.

Hales 🪶

Hales is a small village of about 100 inhabitants, situated 3 miles east of Market Drayton. In the past Hales was an entire estate and except for the vicarage, every house or farm belonged to the squire, who lived in Hales Hall, and everyone worked for him. There was a church and vicarage, a school, a village social club and a shop. Now only the church and club are functioning, many houses are privately owned and the present day inhabitants have a wide range of jobs.

Hales Hall was built in 1806. It is a magnificent Georgian house in a delightful situation overlooking the river Coalbrook with unsurpassable views. A previous squire of Hales, the Rev Alexander Buchanon, finding no church in his squirearchy, since the original wooden church had been destroyed by fire, paid for a church to be built in 1856. The church of St Mary is in a neat pseudo-Gothic style with tower, nave and chancel, built in local sandstone. The silver originates from the little wooden church and the paten, goblet and two chalices have 1833 and the the Buchanon crest on them. The church was designed by George Gilbert Scott of Albert Memorial and St Pancras Station fame.

Hales Club, where the social life of the village takes place, was originally a cottage which was expanded by a musical Buchanon ancestor to house his organ. He left his wife in the cottage next door and retired to this extraordinary extension with his manservant. The organ was placed in a huge panelled room under which was a cellar connected to the main room by a spiral iron stairway.

In a large field just off the A53 and close by the Hemp Mill Brook, lies Audley's Cross, where Lord Audley, the great military hero of Staffordshire commanding the Lancastrian army, was mortally wounded in the second battle of the Wars of the Roses. The original wooden cross was replaced in 1765 by a stone one and is in a shocking state of disrepair. Its inscription, now eroded by weather and lack of care, used to read: 'On this spot was fought the Battle of Blore Heath in 1459'.

The Glasshouse lies on the east side of Hales and on the village boundary with Broughton. The subject of glassmaking in this area is long forgotten, but it is evident that the glass industry flourished hereabouts in the Middle Ages. One important Hales site was at Glass House Farm which dates from about 1550.

Burnt Wood, the largest acreage of woodland belonging to the Hall estate, was originally part of the Forest of Blore. It was named because of the charcoal which was made to provide the fuel for making the glass, and to this day there is evidence of the charcoal lying in heaps just under the surface within the wood itself.

Hammerwich

Although situated three miles from Lichfield and across the road from its well known neighbour Burntwood, few people have heard of Hammerwich.

The church stands proudly on the skyline overlooking the village and is visible for miles around. It stands on a site once used by pagan sun-worshippers. A Saxon church on the hill at Hammerwich is entered in the Domesday Book. The present church of St John the Baptist was commissioned in 1872 by the Reverend Robert Gordon, brother of Gordon of Khartoum.

Nearby, another prominent landmark is a 200 year old windmill. Although now a private residence it was built by Squire Speedwell and was in its heyday reputedly the largest working mill in the Midlands.

In 1851 there were 239 people living in Hammerwich. However, when the Marquis of Anglesey, a wealthy landowner living at Beaudesert Hall, had a coal mine sunk at Hammerwich there was a rapid increase in population. The pit was known as the Hammerwich No.1 pit and was nicknamed 'The Marquis'. Although it had a comparatively short working life and closed in 1865 the population of the village had risen to over 1,000. There were frequent pit accidents due to gas, an influx of water, unexpected roof falls, collapse of roof timbers and shearing haulage cables.

In order to cope with these the Rev Gordon set about building a hospital. Partly financed by the church, the mine owners and the miners (who contributed 1d per week from their wages), the Hammerwich Hospital was built in 1881.

Initially there was a Dame school in Hammerwich. This was followed by another of the Rev Gordon's projects, the formation and church funding of Hammerwich Primary school. This traditional, well loved,

Victorian institution managed to celebrate its centenary before becoming another statistic in the village school closure epidemic of the early 1980s.

Hammerwich has always been a farming community, although today there are fewer farms and more specialisation. No longer are there the farms where ducks, geese, hens, dogs and cats roam the farmyard and work horses, when not pulling the plough, grazed in the fields. Up to 20 years ago a herd of cows were walked down the road to pasture after milking and back again for evening milking, but this had to stop. Driving cows down the road with a stream of impatient motorists bringing up the rear was anything but pleasant!

Present day amenities include a post office and the Community Centre opposite, which is housed in the old Primary school building. It opens for coffee and cakes every Thursday morning, in order that the senior citizens of Hammerwich, after collecting their pensions, can enjoy a sit down and chat with their friends. What a lovely new tradition!

Hamstall Ridware 🎵

An attractive village on the river Blythe near the Trent and five miles east of Rugeley. From old English it is the homestead, 'Hamstall', of the river people, 'Rydware'.

The beautiful 12th century church is built on higher ground by the Manor House, Hamstall Hall. The church, originally Norman, developed over the years and was enlarged mainly in the 14th and 15th centuries. Church and Hall grew up together. The manor was held by Edmund, a Saxon freeman, in the reign of Edward the Confessor. About 1086 it was held by the de Rydware family. The Leigh family acquired it in about 1601 and it remained with them until the 1920s when the land was sold piecemeal, mainly to the then tenants. Hamstall Ridware is a conservation area with 'pepper pot' gateways, a watch tower and walls still standing, all from the old 16th century Hall

The parish church of St Michael and All Angels contains much history. There are early coats of arms of families who have held the manor. There are parts of an ancient tomb said to be of a de Rydware who was a priest. On the Cotton table tomb near the altar are shields with family crests of some 15 children of John Cotton.

Dug up by a local farmer in 1817 not far from the church, after having been hidden probably at the time of the Civil War, were the famous 1350 parcel gilt Hamstall Ridware chalice and paten, unique of their type. They are now on loan from Hamstall church to St Mary's Centre in Lichfield.

One rector of Hamstall was Edward Cooper. He was a member of the Leigh family and was uncle to Jane Austen. Jane visited Hamstall rectory, picking her time when Mrs Cooper who had many children was not expecting a baby.

It is a friendly parish with some old buildings, some renovated and some new. At one time the population was larger than the present 290. It was virtually self-sufficient although it had a good regular bus service to neighbouring towns. The parish is still mainly farming, although the number employed in farming has decreased. Sadly the school has gone, being replaced by three houses.

Despite this the parish keeps its village atmosphere with original inhabitants and new parishioners combining in parish activities. The attractive but now the only, village shop which is also the post office welcomes all. There is one pub The Shoulder of Mutton, a friendly place to meet and have a meal. Although the football team has gone there is still occasionally a tug-o-war over the river.

Hanbury

This small village is situated west of Tutbury, with the valley of the river Dove to the north and Needwood Forest to the south.

The church is dedicated to St Werburgh, whose shrine is in Chester cathedral and who was prioress of a nunnery founded here in AD 680. The church is well worth a visit, set high on a hill. It was extensively rebuilt during the 19th century but there are some interesting tombs and memorials – including the busts of two rather disapproving Puritan ladies, Mrs Agarde and her daughter, above the vicar's stall.

Other castastrophes may have struck the village over the centuries, but to modern villagers none was so terrible as the day when 4000 tons of stored bombs exploded without warning under the hill. Those who were there will never forget 27th November 1944. The explosion left a crater 800 yards long, 300 yards wide and 150 feet deep. There were many casualties, including villagers, RAF personnel and Italian prisioners of war. Huge trees were flung through the air, as were massive gypsum boulders. The mid-day sky became as black as night as soil, stones and clods of grassy earth rained down.

It was more than 10 weeks before the search for bodies was finally abandoned, with 70 dead or missing. The crater is still there, no longer looking as one observer said, 'like a replica of Passchendaele', but soft and green, its sides clothed with trees. Over the years nature has wrought her magic to heal the scars on the hillside and where once was horror and destruction there is now peace and tranquillity.

Hanchurch 🌿

Hanchurch is a small village on a ridge of land which stands behind Trentham Gardens and Park. It is mentioned in the Domesday Book as Hancese, 'cese' being the Anglo-Saxon for church. 'Han' may be high or may represent the Welsh 'hen', meaning old.

The church stood on the site of Hanchurch Yews, and local legend says it was carried down the hill by four white swans. It is believed the church was dedicated to All Saints and at the time of the restoration of the church at Trentham in the 12th century the two churches were united, the old dedication being preserved in St Mary and All Saints. There is now a chapel, converted from a barn, on the opposite side of the lane. The stained glass east window is dedicated to E J Edwards, 1884.

The village stands on what was the coach road from Derby, through Trentham, to Chester. The tollgate cottage was demolished in the 1970s.

The present population of 114 has varied little from the 1881 census of 119, when the village was part of the Sutherland estate. The cottages were occupied by estate workers, including two blacksmiths, five carpenters and a saddler. In the late 18th century three cottages were converted into what is now the manor, for the estate manager.

There is now a conservation order on the ridge, so further building is restricted. A number of buildings, including Village Farm and outbuildings, are Grade II listed.

A local farmer, Mr R Sant, of the Model Farm, is expanding Hanchurch Pools into a string of ten to provide trout and coarse fishing, and landscaping the surrounding area. Two hundred trees have been planted and more are planned.

In 1964 the M6 motorway was brought through the valley below the village and Junction 15 is only a quarter of a mile away. In the valley is ribbon development of semi-detached houses built around 1920. Here too is the village hall, rebuilt in 1987 to replace the 35 year old 'temporary' wooden hall. It is extensively used by villagers.

Harlaston 🐾

Harlaston is a small village lying on the left bank of the river Mease which is very popular with fishermen and is chiefly a farming area. It was mentioned in the Domesday Book, due to some extent to the existence of a corn mill. In 1845 records indicate there were 221 inhabitants; today's population is about 350.

St Matthew's church stands in the middle of the village, and although the exact date of origin is not known, it is suggested that it is Saxon and parts date back to the 9th century. Students often visit to study the fine beamed roof as a typical example of vernacular architecture, while the east window depicts the Ascension, but with *twelve* disciples.

Opposite the church is the village store and post office and a few yards down Main Road the White Lion Inn stands on the unusual triangle with roads running on three sides. Many years ago there was also a toll gate at this point.

The first school was built in 1851 at a cost of £108. This closed in 1940 when a new school opened, but declining numbers forced this to close in 1985 and it is now used as the village hall. The headmistress during the 1930s was one of the first ladies to own and ride a motor cycle combination.

The manor house dates back to 1540 and after many years of neglect has been restored as a Grade II building of historical interest. Other houses of interest include The Homestead, built in 1773 by a collar and harness maker and it is also believed that in the early years it served as the village pub known as The Whip and Saddle. To the present day, six generations of the Mercer family have lived at The Homestead.

Harlaston is very well known for its herds of Large White pigs and pedigree cows, and one of the village's most popular inhabitants is Mr

90

Percy Wallis who has worked for three generations of Mercers at Manor Farm. In 1982 Mr Wallis was awarded the British Empire Medal for services to agriculture.

The village has twice won the Best Kept Village award and twice been placed second. It is a designated conservation area and building is very carefully planned.

Hartshill ✎

Situated midway between the towns of Stoke-on-Trent and Newcastle-under-Lyme lies Hartshill. Although always busy and bustling (Hartshill lies on a main thoroughfare) it has managed to retain its own individual character.

In the mid 1800s Hartshill was mainly farming land, but the comparative isolation of the village and its commanding position (over 500 feet above sea level) attracted a number of wealthy residents, anxious to escape from the towns where they made their money. The large houses they occupied were in sharp contrast to those occupied by their workers.

Herbert Minton, a successful china manufacturer, moved into Longfield Cottage (now the Orthopaedic hospital) between 1842 and 1852. He financed the building of the church, parsonage, school and schoolmaster's house, and a row of eight houses built in 1857 for workers employed in his earthenware factory in Stoke. These are known today as the Minton cottages.

Joseph Spode was also a highly successful pottery manufacturer who lived at the Mansion House, which is known today as the Mount School for the Deaf.

Just off the main road south of Hartshill lies a major hospital complex. The North Staffs Royal Infirmary was opened in 1869, having moved from smaller premises in Etruria. On the advice of Florence Nightingale the new infirmary was built on the pavilion principle, and was one of the earliest hospitals to be built with this layout.

Until 1986 there was 'live' theatre in Hartshill. The Victoria Theatre (in the round) was extremely popular with a variety of plays, shows and pantomimes. However, a new theatre has been built in Basford only a mile away.

Haughton ✥

Haughton is a fairly compact village with a population of some 1200 people and containing nearly 400 homes. Situated four miles west of Stafford, it straddles the main A518.

In the Domesday Book of 1086 it is recorded as Haltone. The name means 'a town in the meadows', still an appropriate name today despite the development of the 1960s which doubled the population.

Several farms surround the village with two in its centre, one of which has an excellent farm shop. The old post office became a home again when four new shops were built, which now house a grocer, hairdresser, post office/newsagent and butcher.

The village hall was built in 1956 to replace the corrugated iron 'Institute', which still stands today and is used by one of the farmers. The hall was extended in 1960 and again in 1974 and the village has a strong tradition of friendliness and community activity.

St Giles' church is of 15th century origin and celebrated the centenary of its partial rebuilding in 1987 with a Flower Festival. The old school which stands next to the church has a dated stone showing it to have been rebuilt in 1841 and it has now been converted into a private house. The 'new' village school was opened in 1971.

The Bell and the Shropshire are the two public houses within the village. The cruck cottage on the edge of the village was rebuilt so as to bring it as near as possible to its original appearance.

The manor house, dated in the latter part of the 16th century, is a lovely close timbered black and white building. Its barn, now converted to a cottage, has within it reclaimed timbers, thought to have come from sailing ships.

The Moat House, situated next to the garage, used to be haunted by a ladies maid, who always kept one room dust free!

Hilderstone ✥

Hilderstone is a small village with a population of about 400, set amid beautiful scenery with the Wrekin in Shropshire to be seen from several points and even a sight of the Welsh hills on a clear day. It is an old village which at the time of the Norman Conquest was known as Hulduvestune, the word being derived from a person's name – Hildewulf, meaning 'warrior wolf', Ton or tune being the word for an enclosure, hence Hildewulf's place.

Agriculture has always been the mainstay of this community. A local farm worker told of travelling to London with a stallion which he was to parade at a show before King Edward VII. The horse was sold and had to be delivered from Islington to Paddington. This again had to be done on foot and as he was unfamiliar with London he gave someone five shillings to show him the way. His reward for the delivery, he ruefully remembered, was 'a bob' for himself!

The Bourne family who lived at Hilderstone Hall, a Georgian mansion, for over 120 years, gave the village both its church and the school. The church, built in 1827, has a unique enamelled glass east window.

William Meath Baker, son of Hilderstone's first vicar, later moved to Gloucestershire, where he became friendly with a then unknown piano teacher, who later became well known as Sir Edward Elgar. Mr Baker is said to have inspired the Fourth Movement of the *Enigma Variations*.

Methodism came to the village in 1791 when a house was registered for the use of dissenters.

In 1821 Thomas Sargant left in his will the use of his house to the Methodist Connection for six years, to be used for the purpose of preaching, teaching, exhorting, singing and praying and the preachers to receive food and drink at no cost to themselves.

Himley & Swindon

Himley (spelt 'Himelie' in the Domesday Book) is a small village in a rural area on the edge of the Black Country and about six miles south of Wolverhampton with a population of around 500.

The village is not without history, Himley Hall being the home of successive Earls of Dudley perhaps from as far back as 1740. Now owned jointly by the local authorities of Wolverhampton and Dudley, the hall is set in 200 acres of parkland laid out by Capability Brown, which is open to the public and provides for golf, sailing, fishing, lovely walks and picnic areas together with a model railway and model village and other activities at different times during the year.

Close to Himley Park is the church of St Michael. Built in 1764 by the then Earl of Dudley to accommodate the ever increasing congregation attending the earl's private chapel annexe at the hall, the church contains many interesting features. A focal point is 'the Good Shepherd' stained glass window in the apsidal sanctuary. Most of the panelling and rood screen were transferred to St Michael's from the original chapel.

In years gone by Himley had its own railway station but, sadly, this has gone and instead the old lines have been torn up to make way for a nature trail to be enjoyed by residents and visitors.

Near Himley Park there is a public house called the Glyn Arms, better known as the Crooked House. Here you may not need to buy a beer to feel drunk. Doors and windows appear at funny angles and bottles appear to roll uphill. The building lies at an angle of 15 degrees. Both it and Himley Hall are listed on the Dudley Heritage Trail.

Another interesting building is Holbeche House. Though not open to the public, this is the house where some participants in the Gunpowder Plot in 1605 were hidden after they fled from the scene of the crime, before being captured and taken back to London.

As is the case in many villages these days large old buildings get taken over and used for other purposes. Himley is no exception. The old rectory, school, post office, the Dower House and Whitehall Farm are all serving other purposes now. A sign of the times!

Swindon, through which runs a canal, is a much larger village than Himley. A steel works was once established there but in its place now are houses and a community hall.

A point to note is that Swindon is situated only a very short distance from Enville and Highgate commons, a large area of wooded and open recreation land, which is very much used and appreciated by the public.

Hixon

Hixon is a rather sprawling village situated between Stowe-by-Chartley on the one side and The Haywoods on the other, with Weston about a mile away on the way to Stafford.

Many years ago it boasted the usual country craftsmen and at one time there were at least 3 cobblers in the village, a shoemaker and a wheelwright. There was also a champion hedgelayer who won the championship of Staffordshire Agricultural Society seven times. The village supported four public houses namely The Baths Inn, The Travellers Rest, The Green Man and The Bank House. The latter two are still thriving.

One of Hixon's most famous personalities was Mr Wilmot Martin, widely known as 'The Staffordshire Harry Lauder'. There is a picture of him in Hixon Memorial Hall. The Hall was built in 1926 to commemorate the men from Hixon who fell in the First World War and the real Sir Harry Lauder contributed a large cheque to the fund when he visited Mr Martin in Hixon.

When the Second World War started an aerodrome was built at Hixon. After the war it was disbanded as such and is now occupied by a variety of firms which provide some work for the area, as does the industrial estate situated along Church Lane.

Like all villages there have been many changes over the years. Hixon has been built up and is still being built on and many of its people travel away to work in different areas.

Hoar Cross & Newchurch

Hoar Cross is not so much a village as a scattering of houses and no one can explain how it came by its name. Although the cowslips that the children once picked in great bunches have now disappeared apart from a few that have taken sanctuary on the vicarage lawn, the beautiful countryside is still unspoiled and an occasional badger is to be seen in car headlights. There is one short length of road in Woodmill where, in February, thousands of toads cross to a convenient pond to deposit their spawn.

Up to 40 years ago nearly everyone in the parish was employed by the Meynell estate and connected with agriculture. Now there are few farms remaining and many of the houses have been enlarged and converted by people working in nearby towns and cities.

The school, like so many, closed after a fierce battle between the parents and Governors and the Local Education Authority, but Needwood School at Newborough is still Church Aided which means that some of the old traditions will survive. Where there was once a village shop there is now a busy public house and the church is alive and well.

The church of the Holy Angels, built in elaborate Gothic style by the famous Victorian architect, Bodley, and beloved of John Betjeman, is still very active. It attracts hundreds of visitors every year to admire the unique Stations of the Cross and, as the visitors' book bears witness, they come from all over the world. Liberally minded vicars have encouraged its use for many purposes such as concerts and poetry readings.

The newest building in the parish is a farmhouse built in 1976 and the oldest is the ancient water mill at Woodmill, still wonderfully preserved and perhaps the oldest in the county. There are, of course, many other interesting buildings. There are many fascinating place names – too many to list them all – but the wood, Spion Kop, was planted in the Boer war when the farmhouse, The Gullets, was renamed Ladysmith; Mustard-maker's Lane is now Maker's Lane and an alabaster bath was installed in Bath Wood by an eccentric squire who like to bathe in the open air.

Newchurch, a large ecclesiastical parish which borders on Hoar Cross, has four large farms, a few houses and a handsome church built during the reign of George III. The ancient Needwood Forest once covered all this area and was a popular hunting ground for the Kings of England. The Royal Coat of Arms still hangs in the church. The Prince of Wales continues this tradition when he rides with the Meynell Hunt.

The two main hunting lodges within Newchuch are Yoxall Lodge – once home of the Gisborne family and rebuilt in 1951 as a farmhouse, and Byrkley Lodge. This large mansion was the home of the Bass family until it was pulled down in 1952, thus ending the Bass patronage of the Newchurch living. A war-time aerodrome was built on part of this estate – still sometimes used by small private aircraft – and a garden centre now occupies the old kitchen gardens. The parish is flanked by Duchy of Lancaster land, owned by HM The Queen.

Hollington

Hollington is situated on a ridge which is about 700 feet above sea level and commands extensive views over the Dove valley of up to 40 miles which, while delightful in summer, means a somewhat windswept winter climate prevails. The village is scattered along the Rocester/Tean road in a haphazard sort of way so there is no real centre to it. However the post office/general store, phone box and village hall are all together and equidistant from each end of the village so they tend to be the focal point to which people and activities gravitate.

Most of the buildings are made of local stone from blocks 10 to 14 inches thick by 2 to 4 feet long and 10 to 18 inches deep known locally as 'shoddies'. Until fairly recent times the major source of employment was agriculture and the quarrying of this famous Hollington stone. Work in the quarries was hard and it was not unknown for its male workers to die in their early forties.

In 1836 the rector of Checkley church, who was responsible for the spiritual life and welfare of the district, opened a small school for an average of 40 pupils, and in 1869 a national school was built with two class-rooms. The lovely little church built by Street was opened in 1861 and a great debt is owed to the Philips family of Heath House, Tean, whose generosity made it possible. The church has never been 'improved', its original state being greatly valued by members of the Victorian Society.

The 1970s proved to be a low point in the village's life: the vicar retired and was not replaced, the school was closed, the local policeman was moved away and the vicarage, police and school houses were sold as private residences. Then the bus services were withdrawn and the village left only with a bus on market day.

Fortunately the surrounding farms remain with the old established families providing some continuity to village life. The children now go to school at Denstone, Rocester and Uttoxeter on buses provided by the local authority. The quarries are busy, the village hall is being used regularly and the introduction of 'new blood' has meant more children in the village and has given rise to a youth club which meets most weeks. All in all, the outlook seems to be set fair for the future.

Hopwas

The main A51, Lichfield – Tamworth road, runs through Hopwas, crossing the Birmingham – Fazeley canal and the river Tame, which forms a natural eastern boundary to the village. Houses and the church, St Chad's nestle beneath Hopwas Hays woods. Once privately owned, part of the woods belongs to Tilcon Ltd and the remainder to the Ministry of Defence. Shooting can be heard regularly as the army practise at the firing-ranges.

The tranquillity and beauty of the woods has been threatened on more than one occasion, evoking a protective and often emotional response from villagers, inspired not only by a love for the peaceful area, but also a communal feeling of shared responsibility towards the environment. Little wonder that villagers objected first to Birmingham Sand and Gravel's plans to quarry the entire area, destroying all the trees, and years later to the disruptive trampling war-games played by 'Combat Zone', for which a rare 'Stop' order was issued by Lichfield District Council in July 1987.

When a baby was found abandoned one bitter winter's night, at the end of the 17th century, Hopwas villagers adopted him, naming him Thomas Barnes, after the barn in which he was found. Years later, in 1717, when he had become a prosperous merchant in London, Thomas Barnes returned to endow Hopwas with a school 'for the dwelling of a person to teach the children of the village to read English'. When the original school house became too small the present County Primary school was built, in 1909, and named after its benefactor.

The village post-office is the only remaining shop in Hopwas, apart

The imposing Victorian water works building overlooking Hopwas village

from retail attachments to local farms. The post-office, with pillar-box collections twice daily, is situated down School Lane opposite a pair of 17th century timber-framed brick cottages. Their white colour-washed walls setting off the dark oak timbers, they are amongst the oldest houses in Hopwas.

One of the most imposing buildings in the village is on the hill. The red-brick waterworks still stands, a witness to the time in 1879 when, following an order from Parliament for the provision of pure water, a 165 foot bore was sunk, yeilding a million gallons of water a day. The well has long since run dry leaving only a new fluoridation unit active on site. Plans are underway to convert the old building and grounds into private dwellings in keeping with the original Victorian character.

Once a hive of cottage industry, including basket-weaving from the riverside willows, Hopwas is now largely a dormitory village for commuters, particularly to Birmingham, although with its plant-nursery and surrounding farmland, and its wooded and watery environment, it will surely retain its own rural identity for many years to come.

Huntington

The origins of the village are not known, but the name is of Anglo Saxon derivation, being a hamlet that was grouped round a hunting lodge. It was situated on a track or road that linked Cannock with Stafford, now known as the A34 trunk road.

The community was slow to increase. There were 46 households in 1661, and the population was only 114 in 1801. The sinking of mineshafts at the end of the 19th century and the consequent development of Littleton Colliery was responsible for the expansion of the population and there were more than 300 people in 1911.

Considerable council house building took place between the two wars, which continued after the Second World War. By 1931 the number of residents had more than quadrupled to 1616. In recent years more private dwellings have been erected and this is now a village of more than 3,000 people with probable significant expansion to come.

The dominating industrial feature in the village is the coal mine, Littleton, which has been producing coal for nearly 100 years.

The mine was sunk by Lord Hatherton, (family name Littleton) and developed into a highly productive mine. The colliery was nationalised in 1947 and has since undergone considerable reconstruction. In recent years it employed 2,000 mineworkers, although the manpower is now declining and in 1986/87 produced one million tons of coal. Modern mining methods and the continued introduction of new technology should enable the mine to produce at a competitive price for years to come.

The centre for social activities is Huntington Community Centre. The original building was purchased from the Parochial Church Council by the Parish Council in 1977 and extended twice. It now provides a hall for events up to 100 people, a clinic, doctor's surgery and two meeting rooms.

Hyde Lea 🌿

Hyde Lea borders the southern boundary of Castle Church parish. It is made up of a detached strip of land between Thorneyfields Lane and Burton Manor. The small village became part of Castle Church parish in 1881.

'The Hyde' was mentioned as far back as the Domesday Book. By 1788 Hyde Lea common was ringed by small encroachments and by about 1840 there were a few cottages there, several dating from the late 18th century.

Hyde Lea boasted a school from 1863, but it closed in 1980, children only staying there between the ages of 5 and 7 by this time. The land and property belongs to the Lichfield Diocese and their Education Board has allowed it to be used as a village hall.

In 1881 the village boasted two public houses, in very close proximity – The Crown which was licenced to sell only spirits and across the road The Dun Cow Inn which was a beer house. By 1914 only The Crown Inn survived as a pub.

The Mottes or Moats at Hyde Lea are probably one of the least known historical sites in the immediate district of Stafford. In 1140 land known as the Hydes was passed by Alpherous de Coppenhall by deed to William Baggot and by 1340 it was taken over by Ralph, 1st Lord Stafford. He lived here in the manor at Hyde whilst his new castle, Stafford Castle, was being built only a mile away. By the beginning of the 16th century Hyde manor had ceased to exist as a separate estate.

In 1987 there were about 90 dwellings and 300 inhabitants. There is no industry and just two farms, so most inhabitants commute to Stafford and the Potteries in the north and Birmingham and the West Midlands in the south. Other than the post office there are no other amenities.

Ipstones ৡৣ

Ipstones is a small village situated in the Staffordshire Moorlands, standing 800 feet above sea level. One mile out of the village is Ipstones Edge, the highest point of which is 1,200 feet, well known for its wonderful views. On a clear day one can see the Post Office tower on Cannock Chase, the Wrekin in Shropshire, and the Welsh mountains.

To the north of the village approximately 4 miles away is the southern border of the Peak National Park. On the outskirts of Ipstones there is the beautiful Churnet valley, which shares the river, railway line and Caldon canal. On most summer days the horse-drawn narrow boat *Birdswood*, can be seen carrying its many passengers to Consall. There is also another valley to the west of the village called Coombes valley, where there is a nature reserve. Here it is possible to walk through the Devils Hole down to the valley and wander along by the stream. The views are breathtaking and the beauty of the wild flowers, plants, and woodlands are unsurpassed. Along the walk, bird watching facilities are provided. This is an unspoilt and secluded part of Staffordshire.

The village itself is fortunate to have a school, general store and post office, butcher, fish and chip shop, and four public houses, in one of which is held a doctor's surgery, twice weekly.

A popular focal point is the recreation ground and adjoining Memorial Hall, which was built with funds raised by residents, and formally opened in January 1929. The village also has a Methodist chapel and a very old church, and is fortunate indeed to have its very own fire station, which is manned by part time firemen who are well respected for their professionalism, and also their efforts in raising money for charities.

There are several listed buildings in Ipstones, and some very old farmhouses which are said to have secret passageways running to the church.

The High Street, Ipstones

Keele 🌿

Before the coming of the Knights Templars in the 12th century, Keele was probably uncultivated woodland. Not being under the jurisdiction of any diocese they appointed their own chaplain and collected their own rents. In 1314, under Edward II this order was dissolved. For a time the Duke of Lancaster claimed the holding but after his execution the land passed to the Knights Hospitallers. Under the Templars and the Hospitallers, Keele was run as most other manors of the age.

In 1544, William Sneyd, whose family had been gradually advancing in social status, bought the manor of Keele, where his son built the first Sneyd House, outside the village. For the next 400 years the village was dominated by the Sneyd family until the estate was sold in 1948, most of the farmers and tenants buying their property. From 1901 to 1910 the House was let to the Grand Duke Michael of Russia.

By the 17th century, most villagers were tenant farmers and small-

102

holders, and the agriculture had changed from arable to pasture. Gradually dairy farming became the main occupation. Today EEC regulations are very restrictive in this industry. Alongside this interest in farming, mining has always been an occupation in this area.

The site of the Hall is now the campus of the University. The village has become largely residential but, of course, farming is still carried on. The intensive building by the University round the Hawthorns in the middle of the village has greatly altered the physical characteristics, but happily there is still the church on the hill, the old yew tree at the cross roads and the lime trees along the main road. Keele has many stone walls and thanks to the Parish Council the one supporting the church ground is in good repair.

King's Bromley 🌿

'Bromley, means broom fields on the banks of the river. 'King's' was added after the Norman Conquest, when the land was held by the Crown.

Lying six miles north of Lichfield, on rising land above the Trent, the centre of the village, is a conservation area containing various architectural features. Many trees within the village are subject to preservation orders, too.

In 1227 the Corbet family were granted permission to clear the forest and heath and build a manor house. The estate passed by marriage through several families until 1794 when it came to two cousins, John and Thomas Lane. Successive Lanes held the 3,000 acre estate until the 20th century.

Exactly 700 years later, in 1927 the manor was broken up. King's Bromley Hall was demolished, leaving only the water tower standing. Today the former parkland contains a gravel extraction plant, large lakes, a nursing home, a country club, a bowling green and private housing. Along the Trent otters have been sighted and swans, heron and Canada geese can be seen nesting.

The first village school was built for apprentice boys in 1699, transferred to its present site in 1815 and opened to girls and infants in 1851. This was the only school for many village children until 1938 when secondary education was transferred to Rugeley. To this day all school-leavers are presented by the trustees with Bibles at a special service held in the church.

All Saints church has a lively congregation with various types of services, including an unstructured Family Service, which is conducted by the laity in modern language. Believed to be Norman in origin, it contains a number of interesting features, including an unusual item for Staffordshire, a stone missal stand.

Modern housing has been restricted to single roads, avoiding the estate developments which can so easily upset the balance of village life.

Local industries include agriculture, quarrying and horticulture. But for the majority of the 1,000 inhabitants, working means commuting to one of the surrounding towns.

Built in 1913, the village hall commemorates a member of the Lane family. The post office/general store caters for the everyday needs of many residents. The local pub, The Royal Oak is a well-known meeting place, especially after a local football or cricket match.

Kingsley ✺

Standing high on a hill overlooking the Churnet valley, the view from the top of Kingsley Bank is one of the finest in North Staffordshire. This tranquil setting belies the boisterous past of the village of Kingsley.

In 1848 came a great welfare worker to the village, a Miss Shepherd, who formed a Temperance League, a Band of Hope and Bible classes, as well as initiating the building of the Kingsley Temperance Hall. In a memoir, the Rev Buckley Yates relates:

> 'In former years, Kingsley was noted for its great wickedness and immorality, for its drunkenness and other demoralising habits, for its cock fighting, bull baiting, pigeon shooting, rabbit coursing, dog fighting, and other games of the same character.'

With the passing of the years reforming enthusiasm must have waned, for the Temperance Hall is now a cafe.

Coal mining has been part of village life for many centuries, records tell of colliers and smiths in the early 15th century. In addition tape weaving, copper smelting, iron forging, ironstone mining, limestone quarrying and burning, canal and railway construction have, along with agriculture, provided work for the villagers and supported the slowly increasing population. With the advent of the newer copper industry in the valley, Kingsley began to assume its modern and more peaceful shape.

Set in the highest part of the village, looking out over the valley is the parish church of St Werburgh, which dates from the 13th century and may have succeeded an even earlier one. Patrons of the living are the Beech family, formerly landowners in the district, who once owned Shawe Hall, and gave the reading room and social centre to the village.

Kingsley church has long been well known for its bells and its bellringers. It is said that the sound of these bells, heard when he was walking near Cotton Dell, inspired Father F W Faber to write the hymn, *Hark, hark my soul.*

The present Methodist church was erected in 1910, on the foundations of an older church. Hugh Bourne, who founded the Primitive Methodist movement in 1812, is said to have had a vision when walking in the neighbourhood of Kingsley.

The heart of the village, with its long, irregularly built main street and odd little branch lanes which for the most part seem to lead nowhere, still preserves its old pattern, built during past decades by local masons, sometimes of stone, sometimes timber and brickwork.

Kingstone 🐚

Kingstone was for several centuries owned by the Earls of Shrewsbury of Ingestre. It was sold, mostly to the occupiers in 1918. There is no mansion or 'big house' here. A sketch map of the village resembles the Eiffel Tower with the main road to Uttoxeter forming the tower and Church Lane and Blythe Bridge Road the struts. On one side of the Uttoxeter Road is a modern estate known as the 'Meadows' with 50 four-bedroomed houses which were built in the 1970s. Only two of the cottages in the older part of the village remain, these have been enlarged and modernised, the others have now been replaced by modern dwellings.

The village has no claim to be an 'Olde Worlde' one. The church was said to be beyond repair in the 1850s and was rebuilt by the patron, The Earl of Shrewsbury, and consecrated in 1861. It is dedicated to St John the Baptist and stands on a slight hill which is home to a variety of wild flowers, including wild daffodils, cowslips, ox-eye daisies, ladysmocks and harebells. In May and June the rhododendrons are a mass of pink blossom and much admired.

There is a large playing field, with two hard tennis courts and swings, slide and roundabout for the children. The Tad brook runs through the village and at the end of Church Lane is Kingstone Wood, very popular for Sunday afternoon walks.

The village hall close by the church replaces a First World War ex-army hut. This was affectionately referred to as the 'Hut' or more properly the Village Institute. It was sold for £100 and the new brick hall was opened in 1971.

The school stands on an island site in the centre of the village close to the church and village hall. In the 1960s it was threatened with closure but fortunately it was reprieved. With the building of the 'Meadows' estate there are now 50 pupils and the school has an attractive modern extension.

Another lively social centre is the village pub, named after the Earl of Shrewsbury. The Shrewsbury Arms is indeed handy for the Earl himself, who now lives on the outskirts of the village.

Kinver 🦡

The village of Kinver lies at the most southern tip of Staffordshire bordering on Worcestershire. In the Domesday Book it is called 'Chenevare' which is thought to be a corruption of Old English 'keun' and 'vaur' signifying a great ridge or edge. Various privileges and liberties conveyed to the inhabitants were last confirmed by Charles I and this charter with the Great Seal of England can be seen in the village church, a notable landmark standing on a cliff.

Wool was an industry carried on in Kinver but on its decline in came the iron trade, also flax-making, hatting and glove making.

The village centre is dominated by an old coaching inn, The White Harte, and several Georgian houses are still well preserved. The grammar school founded in 1511 is now a private residence and this restored building won an award during European Architectural Heritage Year in 1975. At the turn of the century the rugged attractiveness of Kinver and its surroundings became a popular weekend and Bank Holiday resort for Black Country people. It was at this time that the Kinver Light Railway was opened early in 1900 and during its 30 years existence provided a cheap (3d or about 1½p today) regular link with the Black Country and the beauty of the most attractive place in Staffordshire. It is very pleasant to take a walk along the remains of this old track, the scenery being well worth it.

Kinver Edge originally formed part of a Royal Forest which gradually became agricultural land. The district is rich with evidence of troglodytes, the softness of the local sandstone allowed houses to be cut out of the rock face. At the foot of the Edge is a rock mass known as Holy Austin Rock and this contains a number of once inhabited caves. A further rock dwelling can be found cut out of the cliff face of the Edge itself and is called Nanny's Rock or Meg-a-Fox-Hole, once the resort of highwaymen. One interesting feature of the cave dwellings is the chimney flue cut through the solid rock. It was in the late 19th century that the last occupier left. Further south is Crow's Rock with the dwellings here being occupied as recently as the 1960s.

Kinver Edge with its 200 acres is now administered by the National Trust to whom it was given by the Lee family.

The river Stour runs to the north of Kinver High Street with the Staffordshire and Worcestershire canal running alongside. A stroll along the towpath is one of many delightful walks that ramblers can take in the area of Kinver and Kinver Edge, well worth a visit to take in the scenic view which stretches far and wide from the top of the cliff.

Knypersley 🦢

This small village has grown from a few farms and houses to a large residential community. The name Knypersley means 'village under the rocks'. In the opposite direction it looks up to the rugged splendour of Mow Cop Castle.

The stonework on the 'road end' of Knypersley First School has part of the old pinfold with a cow's head and rings carved on to it. This was built into the school stonework to preserve it. A pinfold, where lost and strayed animals were put until redeemed, evidently stood near there.

Near the busy cross-roads stands the parish church of St John, donated by the Bateman family, coal owners and industrialists in the last century. On the corner a toll cottage once stood, but this has long since disappeared. The old church schoolroom and house (which still stand) later served for many years as the Infant school. Park Middle school was first called the Bateman Girls school.

Knypersley Hall, with its lovely farmland and trees, was owned originally by the Bowyer family. This was split up into farms and houses. A walk to Mill Hayes goes through the farmland and below is a large fishing pool. Adjoining this is Knypersley Cricket Ground, thought to be one of the finest in North Staffordshire. It was owned by Robert Heath & Sons and cricket has been played there for over a century. Robert Heath was a local industrialist in the iron and steel works.

Another large residence, now taken down, adjoined the lovely parkland and water at Knypersley Pool. This is a local beauty spot with a warden in control. A lovely walk among the trees, wildflowers and birds make it a pleasure. The waterfall under the road bridge is a masterpiece of construction with wonderful stonework.

Lapley with Wheaton Aston 🦚

Although one parish, the two villages of Lapley and Wheaton Aston are entirely separate communities, lying each side of a lane which follows the route of a Roman road. Lapley stands on a small rise, dominated by its church which dates from the 12th century, the land having been given to the Benedictine monks in Rheims by Alfgar (son of Leofric and Godiva of Coventry fame), in recognition of the care the monks gave to his son Burchard who died whilst on a pilgrimage to Rome in 1061. Lapley is mentioned in the Domesday Book, and it is believed that the village of Wheaton Aston would also have been in existence at the time. Lapley has remained a very small village, but Wheaton Aston has grown over the last two decades, mainly due to changing social conditions which have caused more people from industrial and urban areas to choose to live in a rural community.

It is said that two of the major events in Wheaton Aston's history, directly affecting the size of the village, have been the Great Fire in 1777 which destroyed half of the village houses, and the installation of better sewerage in the 1960s and 1970s which had the opposite effect of allowing more houses to be built. Nowadays, most of the villagers earn their living several miles away in the industrial areas of Wolverhampton, the Black Country and the newly developed district of Telford to the west. But having villagers move away to follow their occupation is not entirely a 20th century phenomenon. Wheaton Aston has, in the past, been famous for its timber fellers, who travelled great distances to carry out this skilled work. Wheaton Aston was also well known for the high quality of its hay and wheat – said to be the best in the country – and it is believed that it is from this that the village's name derives.

In the 1830s Telford's Liverpool and Birmingham Junction canal (now known as the Shropshire Union) was constructed on the eastern side of Wheaton Aston, bringing with it the bargees who worked their way from Liverpool to London with their cargoes. Today the canal carries yet another type of 'bargee' – holidaymakers from all parts of the world.

Up to the 18th century, Wheaton Aston was regarded as something of a 'spa' due to the existence of mineral waters and a 'healing well', and there is evidence of a mineral spring in one of the village gardens. However, in the 1980s villagers do not have to depend on this any longer, as they now have their own doctor's surgery – even if it is in what used to be a slaughterhouse!

One of the nicest links with the past is the village's unofficial flower emblem – the Snake's Head Fritillary – known locally as 'Folfallarum'. This pretty but very rare flower grows in damp, uncultivated meadows and grows in the wild in only a few places in the country, with Wheaton Aston being the most northerly. In the past, when it grew more prolifically, it was an annual event on the first Sunday in May for the villagers to pick the flower. Luckily this habit has died and Mottey Meadows – the Folfallarum's natural habitat – is now in the care of the Nature Conservancy Council.

Leigh ꧁

The medieval village of Leigh is situated on either side of the river Blythe about 15 miles south of Stoke on Trent. It consists of 11 hamlets namely Church Leigh, Lower Leigh, Upper Leigh, Dodsleigh, Nobut, Lower Nobut, Godstone, Middleton Green, Morrilow Heath, Withington, The Bents and also incorporates the area known as Field.

In the central hamlet of Church Leigh the beautiful Saxon church of All Saints is situated. It was restored in 1846, with the exception of the tower, in the locally obtained Hollington sandstone. The church houses many splendid stained glass windows some of which are by Burne Jones. The tomb of Sir William and Lady Aston lies in the church surrounded by figures of their 13 children. The coat of arms of the Astons is still preserved in the windows at Park Hall where they lived.

Two schools used to exist, the boys school, now a listed building which is presently being restored for use as a village hall and the girls school, which is now used as a primary school and which has patterns of blue brick supposedly telling a story.

At one time the village boasted 5 public houses, 2 bakehouses, 3 cobblers, a tailor, malthouse, brewery, brickyard, cheese factory, gravel pit and until the early 1960s a blacksmith and railway station.

Of the 5 public houses only 2 remain, The Farmers Arms and the Star Inn. One no longer in use, the Staffordshire Knot, was used by a butcher until the 1920s and even had a bowling green, the landlord being renowned for his home brewed ale. When each batch was ready for drinking at village gatherings a bugle was blown to announce that it was ready to be drawn and the bowls contest ready to commence.

A significant feature which shows the village's age and that it was once part of a forest is the deer fence on an area known as Checkley Bank. A deer fence is two fences running parallel and enclosing a ditch.

The village green is still located at Lower Leigh where it was formerly surrounded by the Old Smithy and the Railway Inn which also housed a village shop.

An indication that in the early years Leigh was an affluent parish are the charities left by former residents for the benefit of parishioners. They are the St Thomas's Dole which is distributed on Good Friday and the 21st December, St Thomas's Day, and the Spencer Trust which has land

and monies left in trust, to accrue interest which is used to assist local students during further education.

The ringing of the large church bell known as the curfew bell was financed with money left to the parish by a traveller who got lost one foggy night on the Church Moors and finally was guided by the church bell. The bell which was rung at dusk each day to guide lost travellers to the village was only silenced in the 1940s.

Little Aston 🦢

Little Aston is a small but rather spread out village on the southern boundary of Staffordshire. Shenstone Woodend at the east of the village was the northernmost end of the great forest of Arden.

In the 13th and 14th centuries the village was called Aston in Colfield; local wood was made into charcoal which was used in iron mills in the village. Farming has always been an important occupation though the low lying land needed draining, and Claypit Rough, now a small wood, provided clay for land drains and rough pottery.

By the 16th and 17th centuries there were many wealthy landowners at Aston. The present Hall was built by Richard Scott in 1730 on slightly higher ground than the previous house. It was updated in 1857 and 1927 but is now luxury apartments, in which the beautiful panelling in the interior has fortunately been preserved. The park around the Hall has gardens and a lake which in spring is enhanced by thousands of daffodils.

Forge Lane does not derive its name from the present forge, but from an industrial hammer mill which was further down the Lane near the present sewage works. This was converted to a corn mill in the 19th century but only the water channel now remains.

In 1810 a son of the blacksmith in Woodend started a smithy in the Old School House, and moved across the road to the present site in 1830, taking on a wheelwright later. It is now run by the second generation of Sheldons making mainly ornamental iron goods, though many of the old tools and methods are still used.

There was a chapel of ease near the Hall in the 18th century, but the present church of St Peter dates from 1874, built by the Parker Jervis family from Little Aston Hall in Early English Revival style using mainly local sandstone. It is a well known landmark in its attractive rural setting.

The first village school in Little Aston, was the old farmhouse on the estate. In 1902 the school came under the jurisdiction of the Staffordshire County Council and, with the erection of more houses in the area, the number of scholars grew, which resulted in a new school being built, further down the lane in 1928.

There are no pubs actually in the village, but many on the outskirts. The oldest houses are around the Roman Road, Forge Lane, Walsall Road, Aldridge Road crossroads, including the cottage at that corner, the Home Farm, and the Old School House.

More recent developments include the opening of the famous Little Aston Golf Club in 1908, near Little Aston Hall off Roman Road, and a new private hospital which was opened by Princess Anne in 1985.

Longdon 🌿

The civil parish of Longdon in the 1970s was credited with 22 Listed Buildings. One item on the list was 'Beaudesert Hall and Grand Lodge'. The Grade Notes explained that the Hall was 'ruinated'. Grand Lodge, at the top of Borough Lane, one of 9 lodges on the circumference of the park, was the ceremonial gatehouse, built in the early 19th century when the park was enclosed and the public excluded. Either side of the arched gateway was a little house for an estate servant. The whole lodge is now a very desirable residence. Remains of the actual Hall diminish all the time, but it is still possible to find a fireplace, a doorway, or even a window.

Beaudesert Hall had a medieval core. It stood on the eastern edge of Cannock Chase below the hill fort on Castle Ring. It was a palace of the bishops until Henry VIII gave the estate and other lands to courtier William Paget, who was created Baron Paget of Beaudesert in 1549. Henry William Paget, soldier and statesman, who succeeded to the Earldom of Uxbridge in 1812, was created Marquess of Anglesey by the Prince Regent after the Battle of Waterloo.

The manor of Longdon reached to Burton on Trent, but the Staffordshire home of the Marquess was in Longdon, so the people of this village were closely involved with the affairs of the noble family.

112

After the First World War Beaudesert Hall was abandoned. Inns, cottages, gentlemen's houses, farms and small holdings were auctioned off in 1919. In 1932 the Hall and 2,000 acres, spread over five parishes, were offered for sale. Castle Ring went to Cannock U.D.C., to be preserved as an ancient monument; lodges, farms, the golf links, estate houses and cottages sold, but the Hall, stables, workshops and gardens did not. In 1937 there was a two day demolition sale. The site of the Hall, with over 100 acres of land and buildings, was given by the Marquess for the use of scouts and guides and like organisations. Thousands have enjoyed this wonderful camp site. The Forestry Commission have employed local men in the woodlands.

Longnor

The village of Longnor lies in the Staffordshire Moorlands close to the border with Derbyshire, between the rivers Manifold and Dove.

The church is dedicated to St Bartholomew and in medieval times fairs were held in the churchyard, which brought prosperity to the village. The site on which the present church stands is probably the original one, but all that has survived from its early period is the Norman font, carved with crude heads and triangles. Amongst the superstitions connected with the church is one where it was considered very bad luck for the clock to strike three while a funeral service was taking place. It was firmly believed by many that should this happen, another death would soon follow. So seriously was this belief held that it became the custom to stop the clock chiming if a service went on longer than expected.

At the end of the 19th century lime quarrying began in the area, which soon became the main source of employment. A candle factory existed, as well as two blacksmiths, two saddlers and two wheelwrights, among other occupations. One important cottage industry was oatcake making, for which North Staffordshire is renowned.

In the Second World War, German planes on bombing missions partly destroyed a neighbouring church and several bombs fell in Longnor parish.

At the end of the 1960s there was a threat to a 2½mile stretch of the Manifold valley from a planned reservoir. Fifteen farms would have been lost and land taken from 18 others. Four thousand signatures were obtained in a successful campaign to preserve the valley.

The craft centre which has been set up in the village is well worth a visit.

Longsdon 🍃

Travelling from the Potteries to Leek in the early 19th century, the Mail coach would have passed few houses in the Longsdon area. The road through what is now termed Longsdon, was usually referred to as Ladderedge.

The Smithy was situated near the gateway leading to Stonelowe Hall, an Elizabethan house, which derives its name from a Saxon burial mound (grave among the stones) on a promontory to the west of the house. There has been a house on this site since the early 13th century.

The northern boundary is close to Harracles Hall, and there has been a house on this site since before 1470 owned successively by the Shaws, Wedgwoods, Daniels and others, and now owned by the Woolliscroft family. Harracles Mill, close by Harracles Hall, drew water from the mill-pool on Longsdon common, which is now a fishing pool.

The southern boundary of the village is formed by the canal and what used to be the 'Knotty', the North Staffs Railway. The line is now used to carry stone from Cauldon Low quarries.

The houses which now line the main road and the two minor roads through the village, were probably built by business people living in Leek or the Potteries, or were connected with the building of the canals, Deep Haye reservoir and pumping station and the brickworks at Wall Grange and Ladderedge.

The mission church of St James was built in 1871 and the schoolmaster's house was built close by in 1882. Owing to falling numbers of children in the area the school has been closed for a few years. No longer does one hear the children singing lustily, as they did when they had a Welsh rugby player for their headmaster, nor their shouts from the playground. The copings on the wall, at the lower end of School Lane, remain obstinately in place these days. The Wesleyan chapel was built about the same time, but sadly this also has closed and is now a private house. The church of St Chad was built in 1905 and is a beautiful and revered building in the centre of the village.

The post office is one of the focal points of the village, being the dispenser of stamps, pensions, food and newspapers, as well as being a mine of information.

The widely used village hall was built as a memorial to the men from the village who died in two World Wars.

Lower Penn 🌿

On the south-west boundary of Wolverhampton the dense housing suddenly gives way to open country. This is Green Belt land, holding in check the great West Midlands conurbation and the parish of Lower Penn is its first bulwark.

Springhill Lane, leading from Upper Penn, which is within Wolverhampton County Borough, towards Seisdon, changes dramatically from suburban road to country lane before plunging through a sandstone cutting ('The Rock') to form the village street of Lower Penn, now designated as a conservation area. Here is a minute triangular village green surrounded by well-established buildings, including a one-time malthouse, several substantial houses and the tiny church of St Anne, built as a mission church in 1888. Prior to that date the folk from Lower Penn had an uphill walk of more than two miles to worship at St Bartholomew's church in Upper Penn. St Anne's is beautifully cared for and still used regularly for Sunday worship. Until Lower Penn acquired a village hall, the church served this purpose too and was used for meetings, film shows and all other village activities.

Dirtyfoot Lane leads off the green, past Lower Penn Farm, the village's only listed building to Robin's Nest Farm. Its delightful name is no doubt connected with the spring that bubbles up constantly at the side of the road.

Just below the green, in a row of cottages, is the old smithy, later used as the village shop and post-office. The shop, alas, closed several years ago and the post-office, maintained in a private house, has now gone too.

A few hundred yards on, at the bottom of the hill is a crossroads, where stand the Greyhound public-house and the Victory Hall. This latter was erected in 1953 by the villagers themselves, using 2 army Nissen huts.

It is very well looked after and in recent years has won several awards for best-maintained and best-managed village hall.

The picturesque 17th century half-timbered Walnut Tree Cottage occupies the opposite corner and gives its name to the thriving Boarding Kennels and Cattery on the same site.

Farming is now, as always, the principal land use in the parish. In medieval times it was within the great Kinver Forest and would have been partly wooded, but there is very little evidence of that nowadays.

Farms and smallholdings are dotted round this extensive parish; two of particular historic interest are both still working farms. Trescott Grange, the oldest building in Lower Penn, dates from the 16th century and is the third building on that site. The land was granted to monks from Coombe Abbey at the end of the 12th century by the then Lord of Lower Penn. Unfortunately its ancient barn is rapidly decaying. Furnace Grange, now a peaceful farm, was an early industrial site in the 17th century when its water-mill drove bellows to operate a blast furnace.

In various ways Lower Penn can be said to serve the needs of the surrounding area. Its two 'pubs' are much frequented by local townsfolk, its waterworks and pumping station serve other parts of the area too and the Staffordshire-Worcestershire canal which formerly carried vast quantities of freight, is now used solely for recreational purposes, mainly by outsiders. The parish also contains cricket fields, a rugby pitch and Wolverhampton Wanderers' training ground, all of which attract people from the town.

Madeley 🌿

Madeley lies at the junction of Staffordshire, Cheshire and Shropshire and therefore feels out on a limb in the county, being as near to Chester as to Stafford. Though only 8 miles from Crewe and 10 miles west of the Potteries, its setting is now largely rural. It is surrounded by softly undulating farmland and woods, rising to 500 feet. The river Lea flows through the village but heavy traffic also flows above the long main street on the elevated M6. The main railway line to Crewe also passes, under the road, about a mile further south but trains no longer stop at the local station and entry to the motorway is several miles away.

Now a village of 5500 inhabitants Madeley began as a Saxon settlement, (though some Roman coins have been found in the area) on the river Lea, near which rises a very substantial sandstone church, dating from the 12th century but possibly on a Saxon foundation. Nearby are the almshouses and the Sir John Offley school, both founded in the 17th century, with the second manor house further north by the pool. These buildings are the nucleus of the present village and have changed remarkably little over the centuries. The lands of Madeley belonged for nearly 5 centuries to the powerful de Stafford family, given as a gift to them by William the Conqueror. In 1547 they were bought by Thomas Offley, a Merchant Taylor, originally from Stafford who became Lord Mayor of London. The Offleys were good landlords and the village prospered. In the 17th century the Offley heir married into the neighbouring Crewe family and the estates were merged. There are no Lords of the Manor of Madelely now.

The pool with its swans, ducks and fishermen, the half timbered manor house on its bank, the more recent Regency mansion in the park have considerable charm and are remarked on by visitors, but Madeley like many another village has become much more a dormitory than a self supporting community. After the war, three large housing estates were built, extending the village north beyond the pool and to the west.

Reminders of the industries of the past, chiefly of the 19th century, in coal, iron, timber and brick, are present still in some place names, eg Furnace Lane, Mill Lane, Wharf Terrace and Saw Pit Yard. The College of Education, closed in 1981, provided work for professionals and domestics for 20 years. Now mainly service industries provide employment in addition to the Steetly brick and tile factory and work on the surrounding farms.

Maer ॐ

Maer is situated about 6 miles from Newcastle-under-Lyme and 9 miles from Market Drayton, Shropshire.

In 1805 the Hall was purchased by Josiah Wedgwood II, Lord of the Manor. Josiah Wedgwood's daughter, Emma, married her cousin Charles Darwin, the renowned scientist, on 29th January 1839, in Maer church.

William Davenport, who bought the Hall in 1845, made the road through to Maer Lodge and built a stone bridge over the road to enable the family to pass over to attend church. His initials are cut in stone on the side of the bridge.

After the death of Miss Jeanette Harrison in 1963, the estate was broken up, and the properties and farms offered to the sitting tenants. The present owner of the Hall is Mr B J Fradley.

Maer village is a conservation area and still retains its village identity. Of the 32 properties, only 5 have been built during the last 15 years.

St Peter's Church, Maer

Until the 1970s there were a village shop and post office and a wheelwright business. The village still has a private sewer.

Maer church, on a hill above the Hall, has survived many tumultuous times and is still active in its religious pursuits. It was built in 1210 and restored in 1600 by Sir John Bowyer, whose tomb lies on the left of the chancel. It has many treasured furnishings and stained glass windows.

About 1900 Mr Harrison, then Lord of the Manor, decided to build a new school at Blackbrook, to serve the two hamlets – Maer and Blackbrook. He gave the existing school to the village people to provide a Men's Institute. It is now the village hall, run by a local committee who maintain it for the many varied activities carried on in the community.

Camp Hill and Byrth Hill, on the Maer estate, were Iron Age encampments. The spring on Byrth Hill later provided water for Maer village until 1980 when the Severn Trent Water Authority laid a water main through the village.

There are many talented people in Maer and one of the most outstanding achievements is provided by Mr and Mrs Jon Goodwin, who live at Woodendale Cottage. They are both very experienced canoeists who have won many Wildwater Racing Championships around the world.

Marchington 🐏

The earliest record, still in exsitence, of the village of Marchington or Maercham, as it was then called, is in an Anglo Saxon charter dated AD 951. By 1560 the village had become part of the Duchy of Lancaster and remained so until Charles I sold Marchington off. The village then had many subsequent owners the last of which was Lord Bridgewater, who purchased the village and surrounding land for £490. His descendants remained Lords of the Manor until the mid 19th century.

The first stone built church in the village dates back to the 13th century and was known as the church of John the Baptist. In 1743 the church was rebuilt and consecrated the church of St Peter.

In the early 19th century, Henry Chamberlain who had spent his childhood in Marchington, set up, with others, the Marchington Charities. The money raised by renting out property in London was given to the village children on leaving school (a practice still carried on) and to the poor of the village. In 1860 Lydia Chawner of Houndhill commissioned the almshouses to be built to give shelter to the poor and elderly. These three houses still remain in the village square.

Marchington has had its part to play in the folklore of Staffordshire. In the late 18th and early 19th centuries Marchington was known for its treatment of wife beaters. Besides the customary laying of straw at the door of the persistent offender, the husband was set astride a pole and carried on the shoulders of the villagers. If the accused was found guilty by an elected committee, he was paraded on his wooden steed through the village. The procession was headed by the town crier who recited the villain's misdeeds and the latter was exposed to the wrath and jeers of the villagers. His efforts to keep upright on the pole caused much amusement.

Marchington is also known, proudly or not, for its humorous proverbial saying 'Short as a Marchington Wake Cake'. This saying is taken to mean something that is very pleasant but of which there is not enough.

During the Second World War acres of land in Marchington were commandeered by the government in order to build a Military Station. Eventually this became a Prisoner of War Camp for Italian and German prisoners. After repatriation the Nissen huts were demolished and a building programme commenced to produce huge sheds for the maintenance of military equipment and houses for married couples and families of British soldiers to live in. These buildings still remain and in the last few years much of the land has been reclaimed, the sheds have become an industrial estate and the houses purchased by ordinary householders.

The village today is a thriving community with its new school, housing developments, village hall, shops, tennis and bowls, cricket and football clubs plus many social societies.

Marchington Woodlands 🌿

Marchington Woodlands is a collection of widely scattered farms and cottages in an idyllic setting, lying in the shadow of Bagots Wood, one of the last remaining parts of the ancient Royal Needwood Forest.

Although it has no shop, post office or public house it has a fine church, whose spire can be seen for miles around. The church was built in 1859 largely at the expense of Thomas Webb of Smallwood Manor. Before that villagers had to walk to either Marchington or Newborough for their worship.

Twenty years ago the village school was flourishing. With the falling birth rate in the 1970s numbers at the school dropped and despite many impassioned meetings with the Local Education Authority the school was closed in 1981. The closure was almost like a death sentence to the village, as it removed a valuable focal point for villagers and their children.

There has been practically no new building in Woodlands over recent years but there are various notable buildings within the parish. The largest of these is Smallwood Manor which is now the preparatory school for Denstone College. The original manor probably dated from the 15th century and stood on the site where Woodlands church now is. A later manor house was owned by Mr Thomas Webb of the Webb-Corbett glass works at Tutbury (who was responsible for the building of the church). In about 1880 the manor was sold to a Mr Hodgson who wanted to renovate it. However it was in such poor condition that he decided to pull it down and start again. It was completed in 1886 and its design and appearance are said to have been strongly influenced by his wife, who wished it to reflect the style at Eastbourne, where she spent her holidays.

The oldest building in Woodlands is now called Woodroffe's, but was originally Bank Top. It was built in about 1622 by Joseph Woodroffe, whose initials can be found engraved on one of the windows. It was a house built for a yeoman (a wealthy farmer) and has remained largely unchanged. Most of the glass is old and could well have been made locally in Bagots Wood. There is some fine Jacobean panelling and beams made from the trees of Needwood Forest. The house commands fine views over the surrounding countryside.

Farming is the main occupation in Woodlands and obviously has been for many years as the road names testify, Buttermilk Hill and Stock Lane for example. It is nice to find fields with hedges and see cowslips and wild orchids growing.

Mavesyn Ridware 🦡

Mavesyn Ridware parish is situated on the old Lichfield to Uttoxeter coaching road about 6 miles from Lichfield and 4 miles from Rugeley. The parish includes the village of Hill Ridware and the hamlets of Mavesyn, Blithbury and Pipe Ridware. Rake End, formerly a separate settlement, is now incorporated in Hill Ridware.

The name Mavesyn derives from the French 'Mal-voisin', meaning a tower or castle erected by a besieging army near the place of siege. The Mavesyn family originated from Nantes and had an Archbishop of Rheims amongst its members. Another Mavesyn was one of the '260' Knights who fought for William the Conqueror at the Battle of Hastings and he was granted the Lordship of Ridware as a reward. All that remains of the Mavesyn's fortified manor house is the 13th century gatehouse, an important listed building, occasionally used by villagers for social functions.

Near the gatehouse stands the lovely church of St Nicholas, parts of which date back to 1140. Inside, a tablet tells the story of the battle between Sir Robert Mavesyn and his neighbour Sir William Handsacre in 1403. Sir William supported the rebel Henry Percy, otherwise known as Hotspur, whilst Sir Robert supported Henry IV. There had also been a longstanding feud between them and so, on the eve of the Battle of Shrewsbury, the two met by the river Trent in single combat and Sir William was killed. Sir Robert carried on to Shrewsbury and was also killed in battle.

According to Shaw's *History of Staffordshire*, in 1797 there were 465 inhabitants in the parish (now there are approximately 1,000) and at this time the village was principally engaged in agriculture.

Today there is much the same area of farmland but few people work in agriculture. Quite a number work at Armitage Shanks – locally called 'the pot bank', Rugeley power station and Lea Hall colliery, whilst others commute to the Black Country and beyond. No longer is there a village coffin maker and slaughterhouse as in the earlier part of the century.

The village of Hill Ridware, the largest of the settlements, has a shop cum off-license, selling a large variety of goods although prices have altered considerably since the late 18th century when, according to Shaw, beef was 5½d per pound!

There is a post office and petrol station, a school and two pubs.

Nearby in Pipe Ridware is a church which has been converted into a theatre. The Chadwick Arms pub was originally a coaching inn dating from the 15th century, and has a fine sign depicting the Chadwick family's coats of arms. It is a much photographed and popular landmark, often used in car treasure hunts. Since 1986 the village has been able to use the new village hall, built by local subscription.

Meerbrook ✤

On the south side of the brook which runs from Gun to Meerbrook was a long line of earth which was the ancient boundary line. This brook gives its name to the village, formerly known as Mar Brook or Markbrook.

Meerbrook lies in the Vale of Frith, in the parish of Leekfrith. Frith is a Saxon name meaning a woody vale between two hills. The monks from the abbey of Dieu-le-Cres cleared the trees and built three granges, Roche, Nether Hulme later called New, and Swythamley, where lived the lay brothers. These granges were the farmhouses of the abbey. Roche Grange is still a farmhouse but, unfortunately New Grange was demolished to make way for Tittesworth reservoir and what remains there are, lie beneath its waters.

There is a very small village community although Meerbrook covers a wide area of scattered farms. There is a pub, a church, a chapel, a youth hostel (the old school) and a few cottages. Lodge Farm, a mile away, is a freezer centre. Once it was a thriving village with a row of cottages by the chapel and cottages elsewhere; a second pub, the Fountain, which sold out of beer when in 1731 John Nadin was hanged on Gun; a blacksmith and a garage. All these sadly were demolished when the reservoir was made in the 1960s. But the reservoir is very beautiful and has an amenity area, car park, childrens' play area and a fishing lodge. A bird hide was recently opened in a secluded spot at the edge of the water. The village hall, once the Primrose League Room is well over 70 years old and is to be rebuilt in stone, the meeting place of old and young alike.

The original church in Meerbrook was built as a chapel in 1538 in the reign of Henry VIII. Having been altered and improved from time to time so that none of the original structure remained, St Matthew's was enlarged and almost rebuilt in 1873. Both Meerbrook and Leekfrith have some very handsome old houses, some dating from the early 1500s.

123

On the north side of Meerbrook lie the Roches and Hen Cloud, the end of the Pennine Chain, rising 1,500 feet above sea level, a favourite place for climbers and hang gliders. In the wood beneath the rocks is a small cottage, part of which is cut into the rock and called Rock Hall, once a game-keepers home. Before that it was the abode of Bess Bowyer, the daughter of a noted moss-trooper, Bowyer of the Roches, once the terror of this neighbourhood. Bess was by no means a law abiding person for she successfully sheltered smugglers, deserters and other wrong doers from the authorities.

In 1986 Meerbrook was entered for the first time in the Best Kept Village Competition and was awarded 2nd place. In 1987 the village was awarded joint first place.

Mile Oak 🍃

Mile Oak is situated around the crossroads of the A5 Watling Street and the A453 main Nottingham to Birmingham road, on land that was bought when the Peel estate at Drayton manor was dispersed. Still standing are the Gate Lodge on the A5 and also Burleigh House where the estate manager lived.

The name is derived from the mile of oak trees from Fazeley Square, ending with a splendid specimen which gave the name to the Mile Oak Hotel, built by Bass Breweries in 1932. Behind the hotel a first class bowling green was laid. The Warren built adjacent to the hotel was a dance hall.

Before the 1930s there were few houses in the woodland and pasture, just two farm cottages on the junction, a toll house half a mile towards Sutton and Beacon House on the Sutton Road. After 1930, the village started to evolve, when the council built an estate to house a mining and farming community.

Wooden holiday cottages were built on the field that sloped towards Bourne Brook, mostly by people from Birmingham attracted by the rural scene. The land was purchased for 6d per square yard. These dwellings were later replaced by individually styled houses.

Diagonally opposite the hotel a garage business and cafe started, selling originally cycle parts and repairs, carbide, and petrol from barrels before pumps were installed. The site was developed and established a

124

good reputation for home made icecream and cooking. In 1986 the area became a small business park, with an impressive Monarch garage and several other thriving businesses.

In 1963 St Barnabas was dedicated as a church hall and Sunday school by Arthur Stretton, Lord Bishop of Lichfield. The building is used for regular worship by C of E and Methodists alike, as well as by local organisations. Money was raised by public subscription to build a Community Centre, which is used for all sorts of community activities as well as weddings and parties.

Milwich 🌿

Milwich lies on the B5027, between Uttoxeter and Stone, in undulating countryside. The Hall, a pleasant timber framed house built in about 1600, was built on or near the site of a Saxon hall, which was encircled by a protective moat. The settlement at Milwich probably began as a dairy farm but soon included a watermill and it is from the two that the village gets its name. Before 1066 Saxons called Swain and Rafwin farmed the land, then it became a Norman manor, one of many held by Robert de Stafford. There is still a Manor Farm here, farmed by three generations of the same family.

In 1977 there were 409 inhabitants, which in the village included 50 houses, 4 farms and a pub, the Green Man. Most people now work outside the village, although agriculture is still important to the area.

Along Church Lane, All Saints church possesses what is probably the oldest bell in Staffordshire, made in 1409 by John of Colsale. The church itself is Perpendicular, with a nave of purple brick which dates from 1792. Nearby stands the Victorian vicarage. The village school, a neat little building, was opened in 1833.

Fifty or sixty years ago hens clucked and scratched in the main road and children played in 'the Square', the bit of wide road in front of the pub and the old tollhouse where the road goes off to Stafford. Twice a day the cattle from the Corner House and the High House wandered across to be watered at the brook. The forge was always busy, with horses to be shod and farm implements to be repaired. Times have changed, but they still live on in the memories of many who have spent all their lives in the village.

Moddershall ❧

Set among the hills that rise from the Trent valley north-east of Stone, is the pretty village of Moddershall.

While it is for the watermills along the little Scotch Brook that the area is most renowned, the village straggles pleasingly along the lane with many ancient farms and cottages in orange-red brick with black tile roofs. Some of the farms still retain their original buildings around traditional stone paved yards. The old manor house is now used as riding stables, and the small school, which for many years served also as a church, is closed. The few children of the village travel to schools in Oulton or Stone.

All Saints' church was erected in 1903 as the gift of the three daughters of Mr Hensleigh Wedgwood. It is an attractive building of Hollington stone, with a bell turret and lychgate and a well kept churchyard, in a delightful setting. Nearby is 'Idlerocks' a large Victorian mansion built by Mr Godfrey Wedgwood.

Passing years have barely affected Moddershall. Few houses have been built and farming and horticulture are the only industries: two large nursery gardens are the main source of employment.

In the centre of the village the Boar Inn with its duck pond, faces the mill pool where the Boar mill once stood. Not far away is the wooden Institute where meetings, whist drives, and occasional sales of work are held.

The brook flowing from the mill pool leads to the little community of farms and cottages at Lower Moddershall; there were originally three mills here but only two survive, Mosty Lee mill and Splashy mill. An ambitious scheme to restore Mosty Lee mill as a working museum is being undertaken by Stafford Borough Council, with the aim of renewing industrial archaeology in the area. The mills, which once ground corn, were set up to grind flint for the Potteries a few miles away, and were in use until the Second World War. Lower down the valley Hayes mill and Ivy mill continued in operation into the late 1970s. Of the nine mills that once flourished in the valley three have been demolished. Ivy mill is the best preserved mill and is a Grade II listed building.

On the road to Spot Acre, high above the village is the pleasant cricket ground where on a clear day fine views are enjoyed south-westward across Shropshire to the mountains of Wales.

126

Because of its beauty and the historical importance of its watermills the Moddershall valley has been designated a conservation area.

Splashy Mill at Moddershall

Mucklestone 🌿

Turning from the A53 Newcastle under Lyme road to Market Drayton, one approaches the drowsy village of Mucklestone. The first sight is of the church, this beautiful Victorian Gothic restoration of a building which was of a much earlier age. The 14th century tower is renowned by all historians both for its decorated Perpendicular architecture and for the legendary belief that during the Wars of the Roses, Queen Margaret of Anjou watched the Battle of Blore Heath from here.

After the battle Queen Margaret fled to Eccleshall. Legend tells that the village blacksmith reversed the shoes on her horse to give the impression that she was going in the other direction. The house opposite the church bears the inscription

'On this site stood the smithy of William Skelhorn at which Queen Margaret had her horse's shoes reversed to aid her escape from the Battle of Blore Heath, 23rd September 1459'.

The anvil still remains in the church yard. At the point where Lord Audley was slain during the battle a cross stands in a lonely field.

The church has 14 excellent stained glass windows, the best of the Kempe collection. They record the Battle of Blore Heath as well as prophets and saints and events of scripture.

From 1183 the Cistercians from Combermere Abbey maintained a farming community here until the Dissolution. John Offley, Lord Mayor of London, bought the old manor, the money going to help finance Christ Church Oxford. The Offleys changed their name to Crewe and the sister married a John Hinchcliffe. The present patron of Mucklestone is Mrs Flavia Friend (nee Hinchcliffe) whose family have also provided eight rectors. The Tudor timber framed house was enlarged with Regency reception rooms by Rev Offley Crewe, who was rector from 1782 to 1835.

The Keele fault runs through Mucklestone, a geological division 100 million years old. Its clear alkaline springs supplied the headwaters of the Severn, Mersey and Trent and brought Stone Age man here in his dug out canoe (one of which is now in the Birmingham City Museum).

The Devil's Ring and Finger which can be found near to Oakley is one of the ancient monoliths believed to have been used for worshipping. It formed part of a chambered long barrow dating back to 2,000 BC. Women were reputed to have passed their sickly babes through the hole, or Devil's Ring, in order to cure them of their ills.

Newborough 🦢

The village of Newborough lies in the fertile valley of the river Swarbourn. It is surrounded by fields and the remains of the ancient Needwood Forest. Although a few new houses have been built and all but one of the thatched cottages have disappeared, the village remains much as it has for many years. The tall spire of All Saints church dominates the scene and is visible from all approaches to the village. The one shop comprises a grocery store and a post office though it no longer supplies petrol. In the centre of the village the children have a small playground and half a mile to the north is a cricket field used by the Meynell Cricket

Club. These are comparatively modern innovations, but the village, in fact, has a very long history.

Newborough originally belonged to a Saxon called Edgar and was named Edgarslege (Edgar's pasture). By the Norman Conquest the name had become Agardsley and then in the 12th century the village was given to the de Ferrers family and was known as the New Borough of Agardsley. Subsequently, common usage prevailed and the name was simplified to Newborough. It may seem strange that it should be in the Duchy of Lancaster, being so far removed from that county, but, in the 13th century, when the de Ferrers family fell out with the King, the village was given to the King's second son, Edmund, Duke of Lancaster. It is privileged occasionally for this reason to have a personal visit by the Queen to her Duchy.

The number of inhabitants has dropped over the years. The village was registered as having 770 in 1547 and must stand at present at about 500. The main occupation in the district is dairy farming though a great many people now, of course, work away from home.

There were originally three public houses in the village (though many more alehouses): the White Hart, the Buffalo and the Red Lion. The last two of these still ply their trade, but the present church stands on the site of the White Hart.

All Saints church, the 'new' church, was consecrated in 1901 and has several famous people associated with it. Organist Sir Arthur Sullivan inaugurated the organ and the architect of the church, Mr J Oldrid Scott, was uncle to the man behind the building of Liverpool cathedral.

In spring the church is bedecked with flowers when a Well Dressing is held on Bank Holiday Monday. The decorated wells are blessed, there is a children's fancy dress parade, maypole dancing and 'all the fun of the fair'. Newborough Well Dressing began in the late 1970s and will, hopefully, become a tradition.

Over the years the district has seen some dramatic events: a lady was murdered in 1874 just on the boundary of the village 'whilst walking to Yoxall to purchase lace with which to trim a christening gown she was making'. There have been two earthquake tremors in the last 200 years and, as people living in the low-lying parts of the village can testify, there is periodic flooding when the river Swarbourn bursts its banks.

Newchapel 🦋

Originally Newchapel was called Thursfield, an Anglo-Saxon name mentioned in the Domesday Book as Turvoldesfeld or Thorsfield. The name Tur was probably from Thor, the god of thunder so Thursfield is a name of great antiquity and, since place names associated with Saxon gods recall the existence of shrines, it may be that this was a place of worship for our ancestors.

There was probably a church here in 1533 when the first curate Thomas Tunstall was named. In 1610 at the time of Elizabeth I a new stone chapel was built giving the village its present name.

One of the great benefactors of Newchapel was Dr Robert Hulme MD of Sandbach who bequeathed an estate for the support of Newchapel free grammar school. The building which still stands opposite the church was for instructing 18 poor boys to be chosen by the villagers. The school closed in 1877 but interest from the bequest is still distributed annually to students who need a grant.

The first Wesleyan Methodist chapel was built in the main street in 1747. It was there that Hugh Bourne, founder of the Primitive Methodists, preached one of his last sermons on Sunday 18th January 1852. The building was enlarged and became the Sunday school when the new imposing Wesleyan chapel was built in 1876. A new Wesleyan church opened in 1987.

The parish church was re-built in 1767 and again in 1880, and was dedicated to the memory of James Brindley, canal engineer, who had lived nearby at Turnhurst Hall and is interred in the churchyard.

From 1850 the village began to grow since it was rich in coal and ironstone, and attracted industrialists like Robert Heath who acquired land and opened up the Rusty mine where coal and ironstone were mined.

The beginning of the 20th century brought recession and decline in the iron trade and most men were then employed underground at Victoria and Chatterley Whitfield and Birchenwood collieries, all of which have in turn closed down, but the mining museum at Chatterley Whitfield serves to remind us of our heritage. The main street has since suffered from mining subsidence.

Nowadays occupations are more varied with people travelling outside the village to work and some working in the village where there is a herd of pedigree Jersey cattle on the only working farm.

Taking the village into the 21st century, is the Natural Sciences Centre with its observatory and exhibition centre.

Norton-in-the-Moors 🌿

Norton-in-the-Moors was a small hilltop village on the northern-most boundaries of Stoke-on-Trent, typical of the industries of coal mining and farming.

In the 1930s it consisted of one main street, High Street, and a small unmade road called Silver Street. The reason for its existence was that at one end was a crossroads which was the original road from Leek to Burslem, bisected by a minor road from Milton through to Biddulph.

There was and still is the church dating back to Saxon times with Victorian additions, the church school, Home Farm and rectory, the church room and the 'Rec' – a playing field given by Lord Norton to the people of Norton. Each side of High Street was lined by shops and terraced cottages dominated by the 'chapel' finishing up with a farm, a stack yard and the Old Rectory which was surrounded by lovely trees. The village was self-contained, the men working at Whitfield and Norton collieries.

The 1950s was the era of council building. They raised a large housing estate of 1000 on the unfertile fields sloping up from Ford Green valley towards Norton. Gradually in-fill building occurred filling up the spaces at the roadside. Trees disappeared and the old village was demolished to make way for modern shops and a Co-op.

Offley Hay 🌿

Offley Hay today is an indeterminate area, just over a mile west of Eccleshall. In medieval times, the term Offleie covered a large tract of land which included Bishop's Offley, High Offley, and Offley Brook as well as Offley Hay. It all belonged to the Bishop of Lichfield, whose summer residence was at Eccleshall castle. Most of the Offley woodland was open for common grazing, and cattle could be watered at the edge of the lake Copmere, until 1841 when the enclosure act was enforced in the district. But by 1775, maps show Offley Hay as a definite area in its own right, stretching from 'Cockmere' lake at the north east corner to the foot of Offley Rock at the west, extending to the south as far as Lea Knowl.

Today, however, with new roads and housing, Offley Hay is hard to define, merging as it does with Copmere End and Walk Mill. There are four focal points: the village hall, the Star Inn, the sub-post office and the lake Copmere. The land is either agricultural or woodland, the older houses made of sandstone blocks or red Staffordshire bricks.

In Victorian days (1860), a school was built on land given by Bishop Lonsdale. A century later, this first school was replaced by a modern building, but in 1983 the new one was closed owing to the small number of pupils. The building now serves as the village hall.

The main feature of Offley Hay in the past was the heath or common, but this is indistinguishable now. Horse races used to be held on the Hay, and the May games were a great event years ago.

Among the manorial rights granted by the Bishop to the Lords of Charnes was the right to fish once a year in Copmere 'as far as a man could throw a twopenny hatchet'. The last occasion when this right was exercised was in the late 18th century by Weston Yonge, Esq, and the strongest man from the Charnes estate was entrusted to throw the hatchet in for him.

On the north east corner of Copmere near the eel traps there used to be a very high stile called Jacob's Ladder leading from the road to a public footpath in the field. Tradition has it that a gamekeeper once hanged himself from the top of the stile and that his ghost haunts the spot.

Copmere is a birdwatcher's paradise. It has the largest colony of reed-warblers in the county; other uncommon birds that can be seen there include heron, goosander, water-rail and sedge warbler. Around the lake are various rare reeds and grasses; in the woods Herb Paris, spiked woodsedge and toothwort can be found. Copmere has been designated a Site of Special Scientific Interest by the Nature Conservancy Council.

The Star Inn is a popular spot, especially in the summer, where many townsfolk come and enjoy the beautiful scenery of the Sow valley. From Easter until autumn there is a competition and auction of local produce on Sunday mornings, the proceeds going to charity. Another attraction are the occasions when the North Staffordshire hunt meets at Copmere End just outside the Star. There is always a good field of local riders, especially children.

Onecote 🐚

Onecote is a small Peakland village, surrounded by stone walls with the river Hamps flowing through on its way to Waterfall and Waterhouses. There is a neat little Georgian church with tower, built in 1753. The Methodist chapel which stands quite near was built in 1822. The land stretches from the ford to the Mermaid Inn, a span of 7 miles. Some of the higher ground reaches more than 1200 feet above sea level.

The old school which was situated at Loxley Park Farm closed in 1883. The head master was nicknamed the 'one armed Duke' because he only had one arm. He was extremely popular with the pupils because he couldn't use the cane properly. The existing school building which was built by the people of Onecote in 1883 had as many as 120 pupils in the year 1894. It is now closed but serves as a village hall for the use of the community.

At Mixon Copper Mines a dam was made between Acre Farm and Meadows Farm to provide power for the machinery and washing the copper. Later the copper was taken by horse and cart along a narrow lane through Onecote to Cauldon.

There were at least five inns in the district. No doubt they had their uses just like the modern-day hotels. The Jervis Arms is still in existence but the one at Hustins Farm, Mixon, and the one at the ford known as Axle Inn are no longer there. Moorland House in the heart of the village was also an inn known as The Dog and Partridge, and near to Bottom House at Newhouse Farm, was The Butchers Arms. No wonder the latter was given this name because animals were slaughtered there and the meat was transported by horse and trap to open markets at Derby, Hanley, Chesterfield and Congleton.

No description of the village of Onecote would be complete without a mention of the famous Sneyd family of 'Fair View'. Mr Ralph de Tunstall Sneyd of Belmont Hall, only son and heir of John William Sneyd of Basford Hall, married Miss Harriet Brooks of Belle Vue Road, Leek in secrecy at St Mary's parish church, Stockport. He was heir to a family fortune of £20 million per annum in today's value, but having married against his father's wish he was deprived of this enormous legacy. He was born in 1862 and died in 1947. He built a Druid temple by his home, complete with round table and an outer building with many curios – mainly religious. He was also a poet.

Oulton & Kibblestone 🌿

The attractive village of Oulton with the adjoining hamlet of Kibblestone has grown in size since the Second World War without greatly damaging its rural setting. It lies 1½ miles north-east of Stone, is within the Green Belt and has many interesting features. The name comes from the Anglo-Saxon 'Old Tun' meaning an old settlement or enclosure.

Approaching the village from Stone along the road known as 'The Flash', Oulton abbey is first seen across the fields, which were once parklands, on the right. In 1838 Thomas and Sarah Bakewell bought the estate from the Duke of Sutherland, who had lived in the large house for three years, and opened a private lunatic asylum which they called 'Oulton Retreat'. They were known for their advanced treatment of the insane and when they left in 1853 the property was sold to the Benedictine Order of nuns and renamed St Mary's abbey. The abbey possesses a number of treasures including a lace collar worn by King Charles I. The splendid chapel was designed by Edward Welby Pugin.

Facing the abbey in Kibblestone Road is the 'Old Hall', built in 1613 from local sandstone. The Old Schoolhouse, a small sandstone building has recently been restored and appears to date back to the 17th century.

When the railway came to Stone, the master potters moved away from the smokey Potteries towns and built themselves spacious houses in the country; Oulton House, Oulton Grange, Oulton Rocks, Kibblestone Hall and The Hayes.

Soon after the parish church of St John the Evangelist was built towards the end of the last century, it was found to be too small and the north aisle was added. Recently the Victorian porch was removed and a room added for use by the Sunday school.

Kibblestone Hall is now the property of the City of Stoke-on-Trent

Scouts. The whole estate was acquired with the generous co-operation of R Spencer Copeland as a memorial to his father. The camp is very famous and attracts Scouts and Guides worldwide. In springtime the grounds are a delight with masses of daffodils planted by the Sunday school pupils.

Nothing now remains of the boot and shoe industry in the village except the factory wall, the base of which is now the garden wall for the houses opposite the post office. What was once the 'Boot and Shoe' inn is now a private residence. The two pubs standing close together are the 'Wheatsheaf' and the 'Brushmakers Arms', so called because the first licencee was a brushmaker, Mr Gabriel Ludford. Only one other 'Brushmakers Arms' is believed to exist in England.

The land in Kibblestone and Oulton slopes steeply down to the little 'Scotch Brook'. In its short length the brook passes through some of the most attractive and dramatic scenery in Mid-Staffordshire with wooded gorges and sandstone cliffs. In its course of only 3 miles the brook powered 9 watermills of which 4 are in Oulton. In 1979 the valley was designated a conservation area in order to protect its unique character as part of the national heritage.

Penkridge

Penkridge is a large village of about 8,500 people, having greatly increased in size over the last two decades. The centre of the village is dominated by the ancient parish church of St Michael and all Angels, founded over 1,000 years ago in Saxon times. Inside the church the village's history is reflected by the monuments to the local families: the Wynnesburys and later the Littleton family, who succeded them as Lords of the Manor of Pillaton, and who later amassed a large estate including Penkridge itself.

At about the same time as they purchased the manor of Penkridge in the mid 18th century, the Littleton family moved from Pillaton Hall to their newly built Hall at Teddesley. Local tradition has it that the building of the new house was financed by the discovery of a hoard of coins in a chimney at Pillaton Hall during alterations. Certainly a 16th century chalice and paten were discovered during later demolition at

Pillaton. Teddesley Hall in turn was abandoned earlier this century when the family moved to Hatherton. After being used to house American soldiers and later prisoners of war during the Second World War, most of the Hall was demolished.

The Littletons had in the 19th century left behind a more unusual artifact in the parish church, an iron screen with gates, made from the gates from the Boer headquarters in South Africa. Recent attempts to have the screen returned to South Africa were unsuccessful.

Over the centuries Penkridge has benefited from good communications; from the days of the Roman settlement of Pennocrucium on Watling Street and the Stafford road which was a main coaching route, to the Staffordshire and Worcestershire canal, and later the railway. There was a busy market and horse fair and even a racecourse. These aspects of Penkridge's history are recalled by its public houses. The old coaching inns the White Hart (which Queen Elizabeth is reputed to have visited), the George and Fox and the Littleton Arms; the canal inns the Cross Keys and more obviously The Boat, and the more modern The Railway Tavern. In market street there is the Horse and Jockey, recalling racing days, and a half timbered house (one of a number in the village), formerly the Blacksmiths Arms reflects the local iron industry.

The development of transport enabled Penkridge people to find work further afield. In the last century many worked in Stafford, in the shoe making and salt mining industries, or as coal miners or stone quarriers at Huntington and Quarry Heath. The process has continued with the construction of the M6 motorway. Penkridge is also a centre for schools, with the Middle School and Wolgarston High School serving the surrounding villages, as well as three primary schools.

There is a flourishing cattle market held on Mondays, sheep sales are held regularly and a general market is held on Wednesdays and Saturdays. The village stocks and lock up are still to be seen in Bellbrook not far from the Court House, now a library.

Ramshorn 🐏

Ramshorn, pronounced 'Ramser', is a small village of good-sized stone houses and farms covering about 2134 acres which straddles the summit of the Weaver Hill. On the hill are to be found a number of Bronze Age barrows.

It is said that Ramshorn was one of the first Primitive Methodist strongholds in Staffordshire and open-air meetings were held in the fields in the now typical Bible-thumping manner. A Methodist chapel built in 1897 still stands, now owned by the Brown family of Rushton Spencer who open it annually for the Harvest Festival.

Silica was once mined in Ramshorn but was stopped when the mine workings collapsed. Villagers still talk of the hole that appeared and a farm owned by the Barker family which disappeared into it. The hole is still to be seen but over the years it has filled up with water. A walk on the Weaver at Ramshorn discloses a number of sites where small scale quarrying once took place.

Today, Kevin Quarry, the local limestone quarry, scars the east side of the Weaver at Ramshorn. The faces of the quarry are 60–70 feet deep and one blast can remove between 5,000 to 10,000 tons from the earth. Usually the quarry only needs to blast once per week and, if it is to be a particularly large blast, the villagers are warned of it.

Kevin Quarry, apart from providing employment locally, produces almost 40 different products: road materials of dry and coated stone and powders of ground limestone which are used in almost every industry. They are also to be found in face and talcum powder, household cleansers, plastics, etc.

Wootton Lodge and its extensive estates are very important in this area. Wootton Lodge is a very grand house which still survives and indeed prospers in the capable and caring hands of Mrs J C Bamford. It was originally built by Sir Richard Fleetwood of Calwich Abbey at Ellastone sometime between 1580 and 1611.

Set in beautiful undulating parkland, Wootton Lodge must be one of the finest houses in private hands in the entire country. It is a most compact house featuring half basements, a sweeping stone stairway to the front, row upon row of mullioned windows decorated with transoms and, what most visitors to Ramshorn only see of the Lodge, a balustrade which tops this monumental house.

Originally the houses and farms were built at Ramshorn for the many workers needed to run such a large establishment as Wootton Lodge and its extensive estate and, indeed, some of the farms are still a part of it. Of the few dwellings left in the village Ramser Farm is the most interesting as it was once the village pub and then was a cheese factory before becoming the present farmhouse. The original cheese press was used until quite recently: it was used as a stand on which to put the churns of milk ready for collection before the days of the milk tanker with its bulk collection.

Unwin Farm at Ramshorn was once a Post House. It was probably used for coaches coming from Rocester, Derby and Ellastone and going to Leek and also for pack horses carrying copper from the Ecton mine in the Manifold valley to the smelters at Ellastone.

Old records show that 450 people once lived and worked at Ramshorn but the 1985 records show that there are now only 30 in this parish of 2134 acres.

Rangemore ✿

The village of Rangemore lies in lovely pastoral country, where farming and horticulture are the daily ways of life. Some of the villagers follow other occupations, but none of their activities detracts from the tranquillity of the gently undulating hills, woods and fields.

It is not an old village. In the early 1800s it consisted only of a few cottages around the Tatenhill Gate into the old Needwood Forest, but its surrounding countryside is rich in history. The name Rangemore derives from Ravensmoor which was close to the track of Aleswardesley, a former salt way.

There are many other links with the past but Rangemore village itself arose because Michael Thomas Bass, who resided at the then Rangemore House which later became Rangemore Hall, had need of a supporting community of employees and built cottages for them.

Many past events naturally centred on the Bass family. It was thanks to the generosity of Michael Bass that Rangemore church was built and first licensed in 1867 and this was followed by the building of the school in 1873. His son the first Lord Burton was a generous patron. He added to the original church building and built the Rangemore Club and Reading Room for the benefit of his estate workers. This Club is now, due to the kindness of his daughter the Baroness Burton, the property of its members and under the control of an appointed committee. Lord Burton also endowed the lovely playing field for the use of all villagers. It is used

138

extensively nowadays by football, cricket and bowls clubs and by school children. It has been, and still is, the scene of many enjoyable events – bonfire nights, church summer fayres school sports days, when villagers turn up in force to enjoy the occasion.

Through its connections with Lord Burton the village has been linked with many famous people. Rangemore Hall in his day was a treasure house of fine arts. Edward VII was a visitor here.

The village today is still unspoilt. Except for a nucleus of cottages which house estate workers, many have passed into other hands but people have been careful in the way they have modernised property. A few modern houses mingle with the old but, mercifully, there is no spread of new buildings.

The church clock, which was installed in memory of Lord Burton, still strikes the hours as it has done for almost a century. It is hand-wound each day by a villager who has to climb many spiral stairs to the clock tower. The eastern face of the clock casts a benevolent eye on the busy activities of the present generation of school children in the adjacent school and grounds.

Inhabitants number approximately 250 of whom half live in the village centre and the rest in houses scattered over the area. Some are employed in agriculture whilst the remainder have various occupations and commute between village and town.

The present village stores and post office is proud of having been the only freehold property, having been in existence before the Rangemore estate came into being.

Ranton 🌿

Ranton has seen many changes during the past decades. Many houses have been built recently, but most of the original houses still exist. Sadly, only one of the half dozen or so thatched cottages is still to be seen. The village is bounded on all sides by farmland.

Ranton boasts a lovely little 13th century parish church dedicated to All Saints. The vicar is shared with the parishes of Haughton and Derrington, a far cry from the days when the then eccentric clergyman who lived in what is now Vicarage House, fed the local children dog biscuits, a practice soon put to an end when the parents found out what was happening. The post office cum village shop stands near to the church and the village hall, a hall used for many local activities. It started life as a National school, erected in 1842, but ceased to be a centre of learning when the new school was opened in Stocking Lane.

On the outskirts of the village stands the Hand and Cleaver inn, a very popular hostelry on the highest ground in the village and reached via the narrowest lane, in wet weather the aptly named Brook Lane.

Also on the outskirts of the village stands the 14th century western tower, now almost all that remains of Ranton priory. This priory was founded in the middle of the 12th century in the reign of Henry II by the Order of Saint Augustine and dissolved during the reign of Henry VIII.

On the same site as the ruined abbey stand the charred remains of the Abbey House, a mansion burnt down during the Second World War whilst occupied by Dutch soldiers who were the bodyguard of Queen Wilhelmina of Holland. The house at some future date is to be restored to its former glory by its owner the Earl of Lichfield.

The now disused Seighford airfield was the scene of much activity during the war. Wellington bombers and their crews were housed there. Two of them were to crash in the district when returning to base, one in a field near Brook Lane and the other in Ranton Abbey woods.

Ranton has known darker days. Richard Tomlinson, who lived in Brook Lane, murdered his girl friend after an argument as they walked in Stocking Lane. He was publicly hanged for this crime outside Stafford prison in 1834. The Coroner's court was held in the bar of the Wicket inn, as reported in the Staffordshire Advertiser, and during the investigation of this murder it was discovered that Elisabeth Tomlinson, the mother of Richard Tomlinson, had also committed murder. She had murdered her husband in 1822!

Rocester ❧

As the name suggests Rocester was an early Roman settlement. A small fort was centred on the site of the present church.

Situated between the two rivers the Dove and the Churnet, the east and west entrances to the village are marked by attractive stone built bridges.

At the edge of the river Churnet stands a renovated mill. This was originally a corn mill and during later years a grinding mill for potter's materials. At the present time the offices of the JCB Credit Company are housed here. Alongside this, stood a stoneworks which flourished for many years, one of its well remembered tasks being the cutting of Hollington stone, by local craftsmen, some of which was used to build the present day Coventry cathedral.

An historic landmark of the village is the cotton mill built alongside the river Dove in 1782 by Richard Arkwright, the inventor of the spinning frame and the pioneer of water powered machinery. This is still a working mill, now owned by Courtaulds Ltd and used for their doubling process. Most of the older houses in Rocester were built for the mill workers, these taking the form of terraced houses two or three storeys high.

During the 1960s the village lost a lot of its character when many of the houses in the centre of the village were demolished to make way for shops and flats. To acknowledge Rocester's history a mural decorates the end gable of the shops depicting a Roman legionary standard, together with the letter M which commemorates the founding of an Augustinian abbey dedicated to St Mary, and a weaving shuttle.

In 1950 JCB moved to Rocester to begin production of earthmoving machinery in an old cheese factory. During the past 30 years expansion has brought much work to the village and now the disused brickworks, the railway station and inn, the canal and Woodseat Hall are all part of the company's land.

The parish church of St Michael was rebuilt in 1872 with only the tower of the original church standing and to which a spire was added later. With the extensive repair work needed today it is felt that the church will again have to be redesigned. An interesting feature in the churchyard is a 15th century Butter Cross which it is believed was erected when the village was granted a market charter by King Henry VI.

During the summers of 1986/1987 a team of archaeologists from Birmingham University arrived at the village and a 'dig' began in the new cemetery. It became apparent that in Rocester lay the remains of a Roman military barracks. A Heritage Centre has been set up in the now obsolete Methodist chapel, where finds from the dig may be seen, with interesting literature on Rocester from 3000 BC to the present day.

Rolleston-on-Dove

Rolleston-on-Dove is a picturesque, if busy commuter village of more than 1000 homes. Many of the inhabitants travel to work in Derby or Burton-upon-Trent yet well within living memory life in the village centred on agriculture.

Though the village has grown dramatically in recent times, many families have lived here for years, some for generations. There has been a settlement here, grouped round the parish church of St Mary and the Alderbrook for hundreds of years. The original name was 'Hrothwulf-ston' – the homestead of an Anglo-Saxon called Hrothwulf, and though the present church building dates from the 13th century, there are records of a church on the same site between AD 900 and AD 1000.

From early times until the late 1920s, the village and its people seem to have enjoyed great affection from the Lords of the Manor, the Rollestons and later the Mosleys. The almshouses, a row of six cottages beside the Alderbrook, were built in 1712 as part of a charitable bequest to the village from William Rolleston. The almshouses today retain their original appearance, though obviously they have been modernised.

Sir Edward Mosley has also left us a monument in bricks and mortar, the school room, built near the church in 1640 to house the free grammar school. This school had been founded in 1520 by Robert Sherbourne, Bishop of Chichester, and is the oldest such foundation in the country. A girls National school was opened in 1840.

The 'Eagle and Child' became the 'Mosley Arms' from 1840–1851, when it became the 'Spread Eagle', which it has remained ever since. The pub is large and busy, a focus, with the Rolleston Club, of village social life, as there is no village hall as such.

The present St Mary's was built in about 1270, in the Decorated style, though there are traces of the earlier Saxon and Norman buildings. Over the years bells were hung in the steeple, and by 1930 there was a peal of eight bells, which are regularly rung today by a team of ringers. Amongst various monuments inside there is a glass case containing photographs of many of the village men who died in the Great War. The Mosleys held the benefice, and took a great interest in the building, until an argument with the villagers over the use of part of the church in 1910.

After the First World War most of the Rolleston Hall, originally Tudor but much rebuilt, restored and added to, and never very pretty, was pulled down. Bits of the facade were incorporated into houses built on Rolleston Road, a site about 2 miles from the village centre, signalling the sad end to a long era of village history.

A farmhouse near Rolleston-on-Dove

Rudyard & Horton 🦢

The parish of Rudyard was originally an estate belonging to the Earl of Macclesfield and was spelled Rudyerd. The area was about 1400 acres of farms and woodlands, with no church, school, shops or chapel. Through these rapidly changing times, the village of Rudyard, 2½ miles from Leek, still remains a beauty spot far from the noise of industry and motorways. It is noted for the beautiful Rudyard lake, with peaceful woodland walks, fishermen perched on rugged rocks and yachts sailing by.

In 1793 Josiah Wedgwood, Lord Bridgwater and James Brindley, the famous engineer, planned the canal system and made Rudyard lake, which is the main supply for the canal. A dam was made at the village end, intercepting the water from the Dingle brook, which was the boundary line between Rudyard and Horton. A miniature railway now runs from the old Rudyard Station site, which is a picnic area, to the lakeside. This line is now part of the Pennine Way.

The lake has always been popular amongst holidaymakers and in 1864 a young couple visited here called Mr and Mrs Lockwood Kipling. They became friendly with the water bailiff, whose grand-daughter still lives in the village, and were deeply impressed with the peace and tranquillity of their surroundings. A year later their son was born in India and they named him Rudyard.

In the centre of the village there is a large stone monument, erected in 1897 to celebrate Queen Victoria's Diamond Jubilee. It is 10 feet high and 4 feet wide and was taken from the local quarry at the top of Hole House Bank.

Spite Hall has a strange history. It was built by a man who had a grudge against the owner of Rudyard Villa, a house which stands on the wooded slopes above the lake. Determined to spoil his enemy's view, he built his house very tall and added stone gargoyles. The gargoyles are now gone but the name remains as an apt reminder of a sad story.

A few miles from Rudyard there is a small hamlet called Gratton, in the parish of Horton, where the Moorland Poet, George Heath, was born. He died at the age of 25 and his friends and the villagers erected a Runic Cross to his memory in Horton churchyard.

Horton's lovely old 13th century church is set in a beautiful rural spot. It contains memorials to some of the Wedgwood family.

Rushton Spencer

Rushton Spencer which took its name from Hugh le Despenser, Earl of Winchester in the 1300s, lies in a valley in North West Staffordshire shadowed by the Cloud rising 1100 feet to the west. It is separated from Cheshire by the lovely valley of the river Dane. The population varies between 600–700, who occupy themselves mainly with dairy farming and transport, though many farmhouses have been converted into residences. A school, a church, a chapel and five public houses all thrive.

The village church dedicated to St Lawrence is a little gem. It was built in the 13th century on a ridge high above the marsh by the monks of Leek. Sited in lovely wooded country on the fringe of the then Sherwood Forest it became known as the Chapel in the Wilderness. Now the countryside is more open, and from the churchyard there are magnificent views of Rudyard lake and the surrounding hills.

In the churchyard is the grave of Thomas Meaykin. He was groom to an apothecary in Stone in the 18th century. He became enamoured of his master's daughter, but when her father discovered the attachment the young man mysteriously sickened and died. He was rapidly buried, but his favourite pony returned constantly to his grave and pawed the ground. Some time later his body was exhumed and was found to have turned over onto its face. The suspicion was that he had been poisoned. His family brought his remains back to Rushton, where his is the only grave in the churchyard facing west, the rest face east.

Earlsway, or Earlswaie as it used to be spelled, derived its name from the Norman Earls of Chester whose tax-gatherers travelled that route to the Earldom's North Staffordshire estates.

In 1745 Bonnie Prince Charlie and his men also used the Earlsway on their way to and from Derby. On the way back a young drummer boy sat down wearily on a hillock and tried to cheer his companions by singing and playing 'Hie thee Jamie, home again'. An English soldier asked his officer's permission to take a shot at the boy, and although the distance was great the little drummer boy was mortally wounded and fell. The spot is now called Drummer's Knob.

How did the attractive little bridge called Peggy's Lantern get its name? The stone bridge, about 200 yards on the Macclesfield side of the Rushton Station, was built to carry the North Staffordshire railway line over the village brook, and has a sturdy wooden footbridge beneath. The

The Parish Church of St Lawrence, Rushton Spencer

theory is that a silk weaver who worked in the attics, or garret of a nearby house passed this way to and from her work. In winter she would need to carry a light, probably a lantern, hence the name Peggy's Lantern.

Salt ᴥ🍃

Although the village is only four miles from the county town, it might be said to be 'on the road to nowhere', lying as it does to the east of the Stafford to Sandon road; to the west of the Stafford to Uttoxeter road and bounded on the north by the river Trent. It is not a place one needs to pass through in order to get to somewhere else.

In about the 6th century, early Saxon settlers found their way, probably approaching by river. They cleared away forest to establish Salt as one of the several small settlements along the Trent Valley. They chose the site well. The village stands on the south bank of the Trent, on rising ground to prevent flooding and nestled in the shelter of the slopes of Salt Heath. The name seems to be derived from the existence of salt marshes in the area.

By 1086 a small community of about twelve families, a mill and land for four ploughs was recorded by the Norman clerks sent out by King William in order to compile the Domesday Book.

Today there is a population of approximately 300, an inn, a church, a village hall but no shops. The Holly Bush attracts many visitors. The ancient black and white thatched building has, in centuries past, doubled as a Manor Court as well as a hostelry. It is reputed to be the second oldest licensed inn in the country.

There are a few families who regularly travel into the village to join the local congregation in worship at St James' church. They come because it is one of the few churches in the county to maintain a 'High Church' tradition and where one can take part in Sung Eucharist using the 1662 Prayer Book. The church was built in 1842 in Gothic style, with stone from the neighbouring Weston quarry.

Sandon ✤

The village of Sandon grew up originally around the church of All Saints but at the beginning of this century, when Sandon Park was formed, it was moved to the main road and is now an attractive group of estate buildings. The 13th century church stands by itself in the park.

The estate was the property of the Earl of Harrowby and the present Sandon Hall was built in 1852 for the 2nd Earl by William Burn.

In the 1920s Sandon was a peaceful community consisting of estate workers, including craftsmen of every trade, and farmers. Sandon and Marston Agricultural Society was founded by the 2nd Earl in 1839 to stimulate the farming community. Cottages on the estate were chiefly two up and two down, with the A51 (then a glorified lane) on their doorstep. Drinking water was carried from nearby farms and household water by the bucket from brook or pump.

Sandon railway station was very important to the village. Built in 1849, the Earl negotiated a request stop for the express through-train to London to pick him up at the station whenever necessary. The Station House, after a long period of dereliction, is a listed building and being restored.

Like other village buildings, the village hall was built in 1905 and designed by Sir Guy Dawber. It is a building of great architectural charm and provided sporting and social facilities for the estate workers and farmers – including a fully equipped indoor gymnasium!

Shareshill ✤

Shareshill is a small village lying 6 miles north of Wolverhampton and 4 miles south-west of Cannock just off the A460. The name Shareshill originates from the Old English 'scraef-scylf', meaning a hill by a narrow valley. It is not possible to say exactly when people settled in this area, but Shareshill and the neighbouring hamlets of Great and Little Saredon were mentioned in the Domesday Book.

Whilst retaining its agricultural nature and surrounding network of lanes, Shareshill is nowadays a dormitory village for workers in the West Midlands conurbation, with the nearby M6 and M54 motorways provid-

148

ing convenient travelling for commuters. Most of the houses are modern and privately owned, but there are a few old buildings still remaining; Manor House Farm, Orchbrook House and Little Saredon Manor have features which date from the 17th century.

At the highest point of the village stands the church of St Mary and St Luke, the most important feature of the village architecturally, socially and spiritually. In the 13th century the church was dedicated to St Luke, but at some time, possibly during the Reformation, it was re-dedicated 'in honour of the Assumption of the Blessed Virgin Mary'. It is thought that no other church in the country had been so dedicated, at least up to 1864.

A well-known vicar of Shareshill from 1860 to 1870 was William Henry Havergal, honorary canon of Worcester cathedral, and also a hymn writer and composer – as was his daughter Frances Ridley Havergal. He composed the tune *Consecration* to her words *Take my life and let it be* which she used in her house meetings. The village school, which opened on its present site in 1872, is named after the Havergals and the school hymn is *Take my life*.

Hilton Hall, built around 1700 and a fine example of a Queen Anne house, has been completely renovated by an international construction conglomerate for their own use. It was formerly the home of the Vernon family, benefactors of the church and the village, referred to locally during at least the last 200 years as the squires of the village. The estate was split up and sold in 1951 due to heavy death duties.

At the turn of the century Shareshill sustained several shops and four public houses. Today, there is one shop/post office, one public house/restaurant, a garage, livery and riding stables, a large indoor equestrian centre at Hilton Park and a blacksmith. The blacksmith, Vic Bailey, who runs a flourishing business at Little Saredon, has worked there for over 60 years. When he started work as a lad of 14 there were around 30 heavy working horses in the area, but now his work is mainly with children's ponies and horses from the local riding school.

The only local industry is still farming, as it was in 1086. All the farms are family-owned, some having been in the family for several generations. Although farming is completely mechanised now, the area is well-known for the magnificent Shire horses bred by Neville Arblaster at Saredon Hall Farm. His horses have won many prizes at major agricultural shows and his foals are exported worldwide.

Sheen 🦚

Sheen – 'The Shining One' – is a small village of approximately 250 inhabitants set in the beautiful Moorlands of Staffordshire. It is mainly a farming community where the same families have farmed for many generations. Other employment is provided by the local Belle Engineering Company.

Sheen is mentioned in the Domesday Book and there has been a church at Sheen for over 800 years. The present church of St Luke was built in 1850–2 and its focal point is the chancel, whose roof is an imitation of the one in the chapel of St Mary's church at Scarborough. It is made of stone, carved and ribbed, forming a barrel shaped vaulting, and was designed by Mr William Butterfield, one of the best known architects of his time.

One of the earliest mentions of a mill at 'Chene' was during the reign of Henry III 1216–1272, and in the 1790s the present mill was built as a cotton mill. This proved an unsuccessful venture and it was later used for drying and grinding grain for the local farmers, and at one time it was also a saw mill. It stands three storeys high, with a 16 foot diameter wheel, and is one of the best examples of a water mill in Staffordshire.

Sheen hill stands over 1,200 feet above sea level and for the nimble footed it is well worth a climb. It is said that no fewer than nine church spires and towers can be seen from the top of the hill and on a clear day it is also possible to see the Wrekin.

The parish of Sheen also includes the small hamlet of Hulme End, which was once the home of the old Manifold Valley Light Railway. The old engine sheds and waiting room still stand, and a large car park has now been built on an adjacent site to accommodate the visitors who come to enjoy a stroll down the old railway track. The railway lines were removed in 1937 following the closure of the railway in 1934, and a tarmac path was laid from Hulme End to Waterhouses.

Two hostelries can be found in the parish, both providing excellent refreshment for the locals and the many tourists who visit the area. The Spinning Wheel at Sheen was originally known as the Staffordshire Knot and the Manifold Valley Hotel at Hulme End was formerly the Light Railway Hotel.

Finally Sheen's claim to fame is the local Sheen Farmers Tug-of-War

Team. This team has been the most successful team at the World Championships, competing for England, and winning the title three times in 1975–6 at 640 kg, and in 1977–8 and 1980 at 720 kg. These results took them into the 1988 Guiness Book of Records.

Shenstone 🐝

The village name in its earliest form was Seneste or Scenestan meaning shining or beautiful stone originating, no doubt, from the red sandstone on which Shenstone is built. It was mentioned in the Domesday Book and at that time it was mainly woodland with approximately 30 households including the manor house and the mill.

St John's church, a landmark in the surrounding countryside, stands on a hill in the middle of the village. It was built in 1854 during the time of Robert Essington who was vicar here for 47 years. Adjacent to the Victorian church stand the ruins of the tower of the earlier church, a medieval building on Saxon foundations. Funds ran out during the demolition of the old church so the tower was left standing. The clock on the present church was a gift in the 1720s from Elizabeth, wife of Samuel Hill who lived at Park Hall.

There are several large houses in the village formerly owned by the gentry including Shenstone Court, the manor house, which used to be called 'The Moss'. It was owned early this century by Sir Richard Cooper who was MP for Walsall and a veterinary surgeon who invented Cooper's sheep dip. It was Sir Richard who was responsible for planting avenues of trees which make this such an attractive village.

It was Robert Graisbrook in his will of 20th July 1728 who left 30 shillings to the then schoolmaster, Charles Savage, for the schooling of 4 poor children, thus ensuring himself a permanent memorial in the present Greysbrook school. Robert's family lived at Graisbrook Hall, no longer in existence, which used to stand behind the present Oddfellows Hall.

The Oddfellows Hall was originally built as a reading room during the Crimean war. Not only was Shenstone the first village in the area to have a reading room, it also had the first savings bank, started in 1818, the chief depositors coming from the Black Country.

There are four public houses in Shenstone, two of considerable age, and in the Bull's Head can be seen the Court room where formerly the petty sessions were held. There is a modern industrial estate which employs some villagers but on the whole this is a commuter village. The present village numbers approximately 1600 people and is growing steadily. New estates have been built in the last 30 years as well as a row of shops and there are numerous associations catering for all tastes which meet in one of the four halls, the newest and largest being the village hall built in the 1970s.

In New Road are two houses with the names 'Defiance' and 'Victory' etched on the walls. Many years ago a certain gentleman wished to build two houses in the road and when the neighbours objected he went to the High Court and won his case, hence the subsequent naming of the properties.

Slitting Mill ✥

Slitting Mill is a hamlet rather than a village, situated about a mile from Rugeley, on the very edge of Cannock Chase. It overlooks the valley of Rising Brook and from various standpoints there are excellent views of the Chase.

Once this quiet village must have been a hive of activity, for the valley was the centre of a prosperous iron industry. Relatively large water-powered mills stood along the watercourse of the valley, slitting sheets of iron so as to produce manageable rods of metal. It is from this process that the village takes its present name. The Chase was also an important coal mining area.

The heart of Slitting Mill and its most picturesque aspect is the Horn's Pool. This is not a natural feature but was created some 200 years ago as a header pool to provide a fall of water capable of driving a millwheel. Nearby stands the Horns public house, which gives its name to this area.

The village was previously named Stonehouse, from the large stone house situated at the entrance to the village. In 1830 the ironmaster of the slitting mill lived in the house and it was his sister, Sarah Hopkins, who endowed the schoolroom. After many years of standing derelict, the house is now fully restored.

At the end of Church Close stands the church of St John the Baptist. It is unusual in that it is a semi-detached building, the other half being a modern dwelling which was built on the site of the old Dame school. The church has some interesting stained glass windows at the east end and there is a splendid carved oak reredos, given by Mary Gardener of the Stonehouse in 1910. Behind the font may be seen the remains of the old fireplace, now bricked up.

Throughout the last 30 years or so some private housing development has taken place, but in spite of this Slitting Mill retains its village atmosphere. Indeed it is hard to imagine the industry of the past when now there are days when the most activity seems to come from the fishermen at the Horn's Pool!

Standon & Cotes Heath

Standon and Cotes Heath lie to the west of the A519 Newcastle to Eccleshall road.

Cotes Heath, originally known as Moorfield Green, consists of Cotes Heath and the hamlets of Cotes, Cranberry and Mill Meece. In the 1800s Cranberry was known locally as 'Baggum'. The story is that an argumentative villager was bagged in a sack and dropped into a well. Luckily he survived to tell the tale.

Cranberry once had its own hermit. He had a long white beard and lived in a cottage opposite the shop. His windows were all covered with sacks and he spent his time counting the piles of money kept on an old chest.

Mill Meece waterworks provided work for local men and still does, although mechanisation has reduced the number of jobs. The original horizontal steam engine and its building are now looked after by a Preservation Society.

The post office at Cotes Heath was originally two cottages, one was the post office and the other was a tailor's inhabited by 'Tailor Tom'. He could be seen sitting cross-legged as he sewed.

There was great rivalry at one time between Cotes Heath and Standon. Boys from each village used to meet on Standon Bridge and exchange insults. One rhyme quoted was:

'Standon men, like bulls in a pen
Hemmed in by Cotes Heath men.'

Now there is a joint school and parish, feelings are more friendly. Standon also includes the hamlets of Standon, Walford, Weston, Bowers and Bowers Bent. The parish church of All Saints, parts of which date from 1086, stands at the crossroads opposite the old school. Much of the land is still farmland as it has been for centuries, but now the farms are larger and the farmers fewer. The parish register of 1851 mentions only one family, the Keys, whose family still farm in Standon.

The Salt family were at one time Lords of the Manor of Standon and also held the Church Living. Standon school was originally built in 1866 as a memorial to the Reverend Joseph Salt and rebuilt in 1879.

Standon Bowers Education Centre was built as a Church of England Farm Home for boys in 1885. Its purpose was to train orphan boys in farmwork before they were sent to the colonies. One villager recalls seeing boys catching the 8 am train from Standon Bridge station to Liverpool for the boat to Canada. Even now some of the 'old boys' come back to visit the home.

Standon Hospital, originally a private house, was opened in 1932 for TB patients. On Boxing Day the North Staffs Hunt used to meet there and the hounds went round the wards before setting off for the hunt. It was closed and eventually re-opened as a private nursing home.

Stanley 🐚

The old-established hamlet of Stanley stands on a hilltop about a mile south of Endon village. Originally known as Stonelegh, meaning 'stoney ground', it is generally believed that the family of Stanley, Earls of Derby and all the other Stanleys, came from here. There is a small mission church under the pastoral care of the vicar of Endon – the parish is offically known as Endon with Stanley. Some of the older houses and buildings are of stone construction but the narrow, winding approach roads have restricted additional building to a few private houses. Two hostelries, the Travellers' Rest and the Rose and Crown, have been renovated but not excessively so.

An outstanding feature of the area is the man-made stretch of water called Stanley Pool, which is a feeder for the Caldon canal. During what is still referred to locally as 'the great flood' in 1927, the water overflowed and swamped the Endon valley, fortunately without loss of life. Used by the North Staffs Sailing Club as their headquarters, it presents a most attractive scene with boats in full sail. Fishing is limited to members of the Stoke-on-Trent Angling Society as a coarse fishery, which includes some very large pike. Stanley Head Farm nearby is used as an Outdoor Activities Education Centre by schoolchildren from the city of Stoke-on-Trent.

Glazing pottery by means of salt was accidentally discovered at Stanley in 1680. The story goes that a servant girl on the farm of a Mr Joseph Tate was boiling salted water, used for curing pork, when the unattended liquid boiled over onto the sides of the earthenware pot. The vessel became red hot and after cooling was found to be roughly glazed. A local potter, Palmer of Bagnall, heard of the accident and used the knowledge to begin glazing common brownware by means of salt.

Stockton Brook

Stockton Brook lies in a valley half way between the conurbation of Stoke-on-Trent and the Moorland market town of Leek. The central point of the village is the meeting of roads from Endon, Stanley, Baddeley Green and Brown Edge, with the railway line from Stoke to Leekbrook passing diagonally under the cross-roads. The Caldon canal passes a few yards to the west and a stream flows alongside and eventually joins the river Trent.

At the beginning of the century the station and the shops made this the hub of the village. The population was small but self-sufficient with grocers, butcher, undertaker, surgery, blacksmith, farms and quarries, two chapels and two inns.

Bunt's Lane was part of the old coach road which came from Norton Green via Heather Hills to Edge Lane, Brown Edge, so until the 1840s there was no road link with Endon. When the new road was constructed the foundations had to be supported by tree trunks because of the boggy land, hence such names as Moss Hill, Moss Hall Farm and Stanley Moss.

Builders came across these trees when digging the foundations for new property.

The Caldon canal was a very busy means of transport. Local children offered help at the locks hoping for a ride as a reward. A section near to the waterworks is called the 'Lido' and is a popular swimming spot on hot summer days. In contrast one winter the canal froze solid and the ice boat pulled by several horses with 30 men on board came to break the ice.

The higher areas of the village to the north and south are of millstone grit and sandstone, being outcrops of the Pennines. There are many quarries which were worked. Most of them have now been developed into housing estates, so areas of previous employment now provide attractive residences.

Golf at Greenway Hall course is popular. The Club House is by the Brindley canal bridge in Stanley Road and the half way point is about 230 feet higher, adjacent to Bagnall Hospital where players have wonderful views to the north. Walking is a delight – across the golf course to Bagnall, northwards through Tinsters Wood towards Brown Edge and in both directions along the canal towpath.

The two hostelries are the Holly Bush Hotel and the Sportsman. The former at the turn of the century was used as a temporary mortuary and Coroner's Court, which was handy for the undertakers at the bottom of Moss Hill!

Although the population has increased with the many developments, the need for local shops has diminished, so within the village boundaries there are now only three – post office, newsagent and antique shop. The newsagent's shop is still recognisable as a railway building and above the antique shop the 'Raleigh' bicycle advert can still be seen.

Stonnall 🌿

The village of Stonnall (population about 1,200) lies on the old Roman London to Chester road, 1 mile from the cross-roads of Shire Oak. At the head of the village there was a Saxon fortification known as Castle Hill or Old Fort, from which there are extensive views of the surrounding counties. From this point, known as Upper Stonnall, the single long Main

Street slopes down to Lower Stonnall, and so into the flat countryside of the Vale of Lichfield.

Lying where it does, leading off the 'great road to Chester', Stonnall gained past notoriety as a hide-out for the footpads and robbers that infested these highways. Shire Oak, then a wooded area, was known as a 'den of thieves'. With the law in hot pursuit the malefactors would leave the road and hole-up in the village for a few days until the coast was clear. In those lawless times the local inn The Welsh Harp was frequented by these gentlemen of the road, and the notorious highwayman Tom King was born there. The old building is still in existence but is now a farmhouse and renamed Wordsley House.

Wordsley House with its eventful past, not surprisingly, has its little mystery – a hand print that appears on the chimney piece, which always returns no matter how many times it is removed. An underground passage was believed to go from this old house to the manor house which lies at the top of Main Street. This lovely old building was a stopping place for the coaching trade along the busy Chester road and there are still the remains of a coach house, used as a barn, alongside the main house.

Across the fields, by public footpath, stands St Peter's church on its hill surrounded by trees, quite away from the village. When it was built in 1826 this was the only piece of land not suitable for farming that the local landowners were willing to give up.

The post office and grocery store and the newsagent and off-licence supply the daily needs of the local people as does the butcher, green-grocer, and hairdresser, not to mention the fish and chip shop. The Village Institute takes care of the many social events. The Swan Inn and The Royal Oak, both modernised, still retain their village atmosphere.

Stowe-by-Chartley ⚜

Stowe, or Stowa, an Anglo-Saxon place name, cannot be separated from Chartley, whose history stretches back 700 years, when the castle dominated the landscape and a herd of white cattle, descendants of the wild aurochs, roamed the surrounding parkland. Stowe was already established as a hamlet with its own Norman church 70 years old when the castle was built.

Although the historical facts are well known to the present-day local people, it is a common misconception that Mary Queen of Scots was imprisoned at Chartley castle. In fact the castle was a ruin at least 100 years before she was brought as a prisoner to Staffordshire. The Ferrers family gave it up as a residence and built themselves a manor house, about a quarter of a mile to the west which was surrounded by a moat. Elizabeth I had briefly visited the Hall in 1575, and 10 years later its suitability as a prison made it the place to which Mary was brought on Christmas eve 1585.

Fire destroyed the original Chartley Hall of 1450 and the second Hall on the same site was built by Sir Walter Devereux. His grandson, another Walter Devereux, descended from the united Norman families of Ferrers and Devereux, is commemorated in Stowe church by an impressive tomb on the left of the altar. He died in 1558 and lies between his two wives, his helmet hanging above the tomb. In front of the tomb is placed an ancient wooden chest with three iron bands and locks. The locks are all different and have three keys, each held by church representatives and the chest can only be unlocked when all three key-holders are present.

The Ferrers family's main seat eventually became the Hall at Staunton Harold in Leicestershire leaving Stowe-by-Chartley in the hands of absentee landlords. Many of the existing buildings, however, would have been built under their direction. Cage Hill House must stand near the site where hunting birds were housed, Fielden House, south of the church, was once the vicarage. The Lodge in the centre of the village was the agent's house where the rents were paid on Lady Day, and the bailiff lived at Chartley Cottage Farm at the north end of the village. The school, closed now, with its adjoining school house, was called Earl Ferrers school.

Roads into the village are still covered by a Second World War bunker at the top of Bridge Lane and the remains of a pill box guard the old railway under the bridge at the north end of the village. Standing beside the bridge is the village hall, built in the 1920s. The Cock Inn, a 15th century sporting inn, remains another popular meeting place and eating house and the village stores and post office provide a valuable service and point of contact for many of the local people.

Chartley Moss is a dangerous bog to be avoided by the unwary traveller. The area covers 104 acres, largely consisting of a raft of peat,

158

not more than 3 metres thick in places, floating on up to 15 metres of water. It is one of the only two major examples of this type of bog in Great Britain and was probably formed by glacial action. To this day it is steeped in mystery with tales of ghostly huntsmen and hounds riding by and certainly various farm vehicles, including a JCB have sunk below into the depths. Conducted walks only are permitted over the Moss on paths known by members of the Nature Conservancy team who manage it now.

Stretton (nr Penkridge) 🌿

Stretton sits back from the busy A5 Watling Street and the name of the village is believed to derive from this fact, ie village on the street. The village may be reached by following the road which runs by the side of The Sery House (a local landmark) and turning left along a road which runs through the centre of the village. Stretton is a truly rural old English village given over to agriculture and so is composed mostly of fields and wooded areas. The most salient feature is Stretton Hall, of imposing architecture and the home of the Monckton family since the 18th century. The family is still in occupation and indeed owns the village and all land for many miles around.

Long ago the main drive to the Hall led through what is now a spinney at the end of which stands a lovely old castellated building. Made of stone and looking like a miniature castle, this was the old lodge or gateway to the Hall. It was in 1860 that Mrs Ann Monckton recognised the marsh fever which was causing many deaths as malaria; she then abolished the drive and had the area drained thus creating Stretton pool. The pool is now well patronised by anglers wishing to enjoy their pastime amidst these peaceful surroundings.

By the side of the Hall and approached by a lychgate stands the ancient 12th century church. The old stone altar in the church may still be seen under the wooden superstructure. Other interesting features are a scallop stone which suggests that someone possibly buried in the church took part in the Crusades, and a lepers' window.

The blacksmith's shop has stood fronting the A5 for many years, and although these days there is little demand for shoeing, repair of farm inplements etc keeps the smith busy. Stretton mill no longer functions, but some of the stones and machinery are now in Shugborough museum. The Old Mill House is now a thriving farm.

A village school was built originally to educate the children of Stretton. This was closed in 1981, but the building still belongs to the Monckton family and is now a preparatory school and kindergarten.

There is no village street in Stretton, just one village shop cum post office standing in the village centre, where most goods may be purchased in an emergency.

In years past, children could safely roam the fields and woods making their own amusements according to the season, blackberrying, birds' nesting, nut and conker collecting. Seasonal games were skipping, whip and top, hop scotch, Cock-on-the-Midden, and of course in winter snowballing, sliding and sledging whilst the gentry skated on the frozen pool.

In retrospect many think that the old days were happier, there was work for everyone, all repairs being done by estate workers. Now only gardeners, gamekeeper and farm workers are employed in Stretton. Tied cottages have now disappeared, and out-buildings and land have been absorbed into the area worked by the estate. There is now a smallholding in the village centre called 'Roses Temp du Passe'. Here old fashioned roses are grown for export. In general appearance the village seems to have changed little over the years.

Stretton & Claymills 🦢

Stretton is a large suburban village lying 2 miles north of Burton-upon-Trent, flanked to the north by the river Dove, and to the east by the river Trent.

It has enjoyed a long if relatively uneventful history. Prehistoric remains have been uncovered, and it is possible that Stretton may have been an important settlement in Roman times. The village is situated on the old Roman road, Ryknild Street, between Derby and Lichfield, hence its name 'tun on a Roman road'.

Following the dissolution of Burton abbey in 1544 ownership of the manor passed to Henry VIII's secretary Lord Paget. Stretton remained in the hands of the Paget family, latterly the Marquesses of Anglesey, until the estate was broken up in the 1920s.

Historically Stretton was a farming community and at one time there were eight farms of varying sizes in the village. The village was almost self sufficient, having people with various skills and abilities ie blacksmith, wheelwright, baker, butcher, tailor etc. According to the 1861 census, many of the inhabitants were employed in agriculture, some at the iron works or at the breweries in Burton and others were employed in service, trades or professions.

The iron works were on the site of an old corn mill at Claymills, owned by Thomas Thornewill who built Dovecliff in about 1790. The site is now derelict. Pirelli, an Italian rubber company built a factory at Stretton in 1929, bringing a new source of employment to the area. Rumenco, a producer of cattle food has a factory on the outskirts of the village and there are 3 small light industry units on the site of old gravel workings in Hillfield Lane. Gravel was excavated in the village until the 1950s.

When industry came to Stretton, a need for more houses became apparent, and small plots of land were sold in the 1930s to meet the demand. Since the 1960s all the farms have disappeared, and the vast areas of farmland have been replaced by huge housing developments. The population has grown from 472 inhabitants in 1861 to over 5,000 in 1988.

The first church was built in Stretton in 1837. A stone cross in the centre path in the churchyard marks where the altar stood. The present church (St Mary's) was built in 1897 through the generosity of John Gretton Esq of Newton Solney, a member of the Burton brewing family, whose descendants are still patrons of the Living.

The Methodist Chapel was built in 1893. In the 1960s the front and interior of the building were modernised. In 1842 the Marquis of Anglesey gave a parcel of waste land for the first school to be built, to provide education for the poorer classes. This was situated on the corner of Church Road opposite the church.

The Trent and Mersey canal passes through Stretton, crossing the river Dove by an aqueduct with 23 arches. This was an important waterway until the coming of the railways in 1848. The line was closed in 1967, and today a length of the disused railway line is owned by the Parish Council, who have developed it into a 'Nature Trail'.

There are three public houses in Stretton, the oldest being the Anglesey Arms, two playing fields, owned and maintained by the Parish Council, three Bowling Clubs, a Social Club, a village hall and a small shopping development.

Swynnerton 🌿

Swynnerton typifies the old English village with its stately Hall standing in parkland, the churches, thatched cottages, cricket ground and inn which once incorporated a farm. Yet, concealed from the main road, a well planned estate of 'executive houses' has been built on the Hall's former kitchen gardens, using its high walls and some original fruit trees. Two neat rows of council houses adjoin. A modern village hall in Early Lane replaces the old Institute, which, in turn, took the place of the men's reading room.

Swynnerton was first built on lower ground to the south around the home of a Saxon prince. It had a Wednesday market and an annual fair on the Feast of the Assumption, 15th August, granted by Edward I. The manor house existed here until its destruction by Cromwell. When a new hall was built, it was on high ground by the church, the present fine Hall being built in 1725. This left the old cottages spoiling the view from the Hall, so they were removed and the villagers settled behind the Hall. Park Lodge provided a gate across the road through the park, with the children opening the gate to travellers in return for pennies. The Hall and estate were the hub of the village for centuries, providing work for the tenants.

Swynnertons were Lords of the Manor from the Norman Conquest until the middle of the 16th century when a daughter married a Fitzherbert, the name of the present Lord Stafford. One of his ancestors was Maria, Mrs Fitzherbert who, when her husband died, met and married the Prince of Wales, later to be George IV. The marriage was not recognised as the Prince was too young to be married without his father's permission, and as Mrs Fitzherbert was a Catholic.

The Fitzherberts have long been a Catholic family and in the mid 19th century, they built, in Gothic sytle, the Catholic church adjoining the Hall and facing the Anglican church of St Mary's. Swynnerton is proud of its ecumenical relationships, sharing several services each year, notably the joint carol service, and supporting each other's social events. The village is also fortunate to still maintain its own primary school.

St Mary's church has a fine Norman inner doorway carved with 16 beakheads, though they could be wolves' heads. Inside is the tomb of a Crusader, John de Swynnerton, and an intricately carved oak screen from

The village of Swynnerton

Tudor times. The vestry chapel where early members of the Fitzherbert family are buried contains a huge statue of Christ, 7 feet high, seated but foreshortened as if it was originally sculpted for a high position. It was discovered buried under the floor, possibly having been moved from Lichfield cathedral to avoid destruction by the Puritans. One arm is broken but the other is drawing back the robes to show the wound on His side.

The name of Frobisher is commemorated by the name of a drive on the housing estate, as are those of a long serving postwoman Mrs Fairbanks who was awarded the BEM, and a local district nurse, Nurse Lawrence. A short row of old people's bungalows stands on William's Walk named after Mr Watkins who served the church as sexton and tower master, dying in 1982 as he rang in a peal of bells. The other row of bungalows is on Bernard Cheadle Close, remembering a recent member of a village family going back several generations. It was a Cheadle, the blacksmith, who warned the Swynnerton family of Cromwell's approach, giving them time to flee.

Trentham 🐝

Trentham in North Staffordshire is famous as being a former residence of the Dukes of Sutherland, or Leveson-Gower family. The estate was purchased by James Leveson in 1540 and the family resided at Trentham Hall until the beginning of the 20th century. By this time the very feature that had attracted the Leveson-Gowers to the area, the tree-fringed Trent, had become so polluted in the course of its journey through the Potteries that the fourth Duke and his family moved from Trentham in 1905. However as a result of having resided there for such a length of time, one can appreciate the tendency to believe that Trentham's history commences in the 16th century at the coming of the Leveson-Gowers when, in fact, it is much older than that.

Evidence of ancient farming methods still exists on the east side of the A34 trunk road at Ash Green where the lush green field rises in the form of an irregular staircase.

However an important period began at Trentham towards the close of the 7th century with the establishment of the earliest of the religious houses to be built there. Tradition has it that this was founded by Werburgh, daughter of Wulphere, King of Mercia. The latter governed Mercia from AD 659–674 and had a 'castle' or 'camp' at Bury Bank some 3 miles south of Trentham.

Werburgh became the first Abbess of Trentham, the nunnery being dedicated to St Mary. No trace of those buildings may be seen but in 1858 the foundation stones of her church were discovered when drainage works were being undertaken beneath the walls of the present church.

Little is then known of Trentham until the Norman Conquest but from the Domesday Survey it is apparent that a church had been built to replace an earlier one which, like so many others, had been destroyed by Danish invaders. It is uncertain who built the new church but tradition has it that Elfleda, daughter of Alfred the Great, was responsible. She rebuilt a number of churches which had been destroyed by the Danes and it is probable that she rebuilt the Trentham church in the early 10th century.

However, between the years 1536–1539 Henry VIII took over the wealth of all the monasteries which were then dissolved. Trentham Priory was surrendered in 1536 and the King asserted the right to the ancient royal demesne and resumed possession. Thus ends the period of religious houses at Trentham.

In 1538 the site of the priory and estate was sold to the Duke of Suffolk. In 1539 the estate was sold to Sir Thomas Pope but in the following year it was acquired by James Leveson of Wolverhampton. As one era finished, another one began.

Trysull & Seisdon 🦜

These two villages have a combined population of 1000 and lie in the south of the county, roughly between Bobbington and Wombourne. Seisdon gave its name to the County Hundred in Saxon times and is mentioned in the Domesday Book.

The mill, a Grade II listed building in Trysull, has now been converted into a lovely dwelling house, standing on the edge of Smestow Brook, but the machinery and wheel, which was made in Kidderminster, are preserved, together with some old Russian pine beams, 14 inches thick. Two pairs of the three original French grinding stones were sold to the Staffordshire Council, the other remaining.

There is also an old manor house in Trysull dated 1653, which has been lovingly restored.

Trysull church dates back to the 12th century and has a beautiful screen in the sanctuary. There was a bequest which says that the verger should be paid £1 per year to keep the congregation awake during the sermon. This has never been necessary! There is a set of six bells in the belfry, the two earliest dating to the 1700s and the heaviest weighing 11 hundredweight. Last year 20 handbells were acquired, dating to 1885 and these are regularly rung by a band of enthusiastic ringers, ages ranging from 7 to 71 years.

In Seisdon there was a bequest from a Thomas Rudge, whereby money and income from lands, were left to provide the teaching of poor children in the parish, in reading, writing, arithmetic and the Catechism. This was called the Free School Charity, and is now administered by a Trust to provide educational outings and Bibles for school leavers.

There is also the John Rudge Trust, which provides monies for three almshouses and charitable gifts. These are now going to be replaced by modern bungalows, still for people in need.

The original Court House for this area still stands and is a stone house in Seisdon.

Trysull has two pubs, a club and a hotel. The village green is a very pleasant area, with a flagpole in the middle, around which, at times, the children do Maypole dancing. Two trees were planted here to commemorate the birth of His Royal Highness Prince Charles.

Wall 🦡

The small village of Wall is situated 3 miles south of the cathedral city of Lichfield. It lies on the old Watling Street, although the village has now been by-passed much to the relief of the residents.

In Roman times posting stations were set up on this Imperial Route where horses could be changed and overnight lodgings obtained. Wall was one of these stations known as Letocetum and appears to have been a large settlement with substantial buildings. Today it is a great attraction to tourists, who come all year round to view the remains of the Bath House – the most complete example of its kind in Britain. There is a small museum containing Roman artefacts and excavations are still being carried out by the Staffordshire Archaeological Society.

Opposite the Roman Museum stands the village hall. This was a gift from Captain Harrison of Aldershawe Hall to the working men of the village in the early 1900s, providing they dug out the footings! The bricks were transported from the old canal at Pipe Hill Wharf. The building was constructed in such a way that if it was not used as a working men's club it could be converted into living accommodation.

Years ago the village boasted a butcher's shop, post office, two shops and two inns. Today there is one inn, The Trooper, at the top of the village which is a very popular meeting place. In the First World War the troops rested their horses here and there was a blacksmith's forge on the site of The Trooper car park.

At the top of the hill stands St John's church, a small neat structure of mixed architecture erected in 1843. It was built at a cost of about £1,500 of which £900 was derived from the principal and accumulated interest of a legacy of £600 left some 20 years previously by a Mr Hill, a local resident. John Mott Esq gave the site of the church and endowed the living with three cottages. In 1982 members of the church and village co-operated to carry out a major restoration of the inside of the church, which not only restored the delightful little church to its former glory but helped to create a community spirit.

The village school closed in 1978 and the children now attend school in Lichfield.

Wall Cricket Team have an idyllic setting for their cricket field where many a pleasant summer afternoon is spent and tea is served in the pavilion.

Soil in the area is well suited to agriculture and Manor Farmhouse at the top of the village was built in 1669. Before farm mechanisation most of the menfolk of the village would have been employed in agriculture. Today they commute to nearby urban centres such as Lichfield and Birmingham. Unlike many neighbouring villages Wall has changed little over the years and still remains a true village.

Wall Heath 🌿

The village of Wall Heath lies at the southernmost border of Staffordshire with the county of West Midlands. It is now a largely residential community and has, since the Second World War, grown to house a population of 4500.

At the end of the 13th century it was a hamlet at the north eastern edge of Kinver Forest. Nearby were Roman earthworks known as the Walls; the hamlet was then known as Kings-Wall-huh, from which it is easy to see how its present name was derived.

Agriculture and market gardening have always played a big part in the life of the village and surrounding area, as the windmill (minus its sails since 1914) bears witness.

The Industrial Revolution, of course, made its mark; for some time industries were carried on, as present day road names testify eg Foundry Road, Forge Lane. However, the village managed to remain outside the area known as 'the Black Country'. It is still on the western extremity of the conurbation and looks out onto open country which stretches away to the Welsh coast.

The church of the Ascension has existed for less than 100 years. Before that, Wall Heath was a very small part of the parish of St Mary's, Kingswinford. There is also a United Reformed church formerly Congregational, the building also being well under 100 years old. Both these churches are situated on the main road (A449) which runs through the village.

That other centre of village life, the public house, is not over represented with only five examples in the village proper. The Horse and Jockey still has its coach house and stables at the rear to remind us of a more graceful and leisurely age. Wall Heath Inn is said to have been used by the 'gentlemen of the road'. More recently, the Yew Tree was a very popular destination for horse drawn 'brakes' bringing Sunday morning trippers from nearby industrial towns; whether the attraction was its renowned gardens and greenhouses or its equally famous ham and egg breakfasts, is difficult to say.

The nearest the village had to a stately home was Wall Heath House, demolished in the 1960s to provide the site for the present shopping precinct. It was however of no great age or historical interest, unlike its near neighbour, Holbeche House, a few hundred yards away, where Robert Catesby was shot dead after the failure of the Guy Fawkes Gun Powder Plot.

Finally, no account of Wall Heath would be complete without a word about the Community Centre, which in a very real sense, is the hub of much village life. Not just housing the various activities involved, but through its Community Association, supporting and developing many local groups.

Walton-on-the-Hill

Walton-on-the-Hill is situated in the parish of Berkswich, to the south of Stafford town itself. Berkswich and Walton are mentioned in the Domesday Book.

In the 18th century, men with business interests in the county town began building large houses out of Stafford itself. Stafford was considered an unhealthy place to live being low-lying and damp. Walton-on-the-Hill became a favoured place to build, the old village being high up. Several of these houses still exist in the old village, those of note being Congreve House, and Walton Bury. On the outskirs were Milford Hall at one end of the village and Baswich House at the other.

Congreve House was named after Thomas Congreve, the grandfather of the inventor of the Congreve rocket. Baswich House was owned by the Salt family. It was built on the site of an old inn, near to the gibbet and stocks and is now the Staffordshire Police Headquarters. The William Salt Library in Stafford owes its existence to this family. Milford Hall, the lovely country home of the Levett/Haszard family, is the only house still lived in by members of the family.

Two major events have played a part in making the village the place it is today. Between 1817 and 1820 the main road from Lichfield was diverted from a course which ran over the hill and through the old village, to one lower down, now part of the main road. This meant that the old village could be left in peace and it is still a place of narrow winding lanes. The oldest house is timber framed and stands next to the Old Smithy. The smith still comes to this venue to shoe local horses. Opposite stands the village pump, and the pound. The second event was the building of the church, on land given by Lord Lichfield. This church was opened as a chapel of ease in 1842, still part of the parish of Berkswich. It is a very pretty church, quite small, and very popular for weddings.

Sport has always played a large part in the life of the village. In the 1920s great 'Cricket Weeks' were held, played on a field in the high part of the village. Later the Levett family lent land opposite the main rooms of Milford Hall, for the use of Milford Cricket Club. The ground was given in memory of their only son Richard Byrd Levett, who was killed in France, aged 19 years in the First World War. Milford Hall Cricket Club thrives. It must be one of the loveliest settings for village cricket in the country, surrounded by mature trees, with the Hall watching over it still.

As early as 1813 a school was opened by the Levett family, in a house almost opposite the main gates to Milford Hall. This was followed by a village school, close to the village hall, which is still in use, although in the 1970s a further school Berkswich C.E. Primary School was built in the upper part of the village. Walton High School followed, this is situated in the village and serves a large area of the surrounding country.

Employment in the village was mainly on the land, and in the service of the landed families. Most people who live in the village now work in Stafford, or Wolverhampton. Some men from the village were employed at the Salt Works, near to the parish church, at Baswich. For centuries salt was extracted at this spot. However, in the 1970s it was found that modern processes for extracting salt caused subsidence in the town of Stafford itself, some 3 miles away! Several court cases ensued and eventually the extraction ceased. The area is now a mobile home park.

Walton-on-the-Hill is a thriving village which has been declared a conservation area. The churchyard has won prizes in the Lichfield Diocese's competition for the best kept churchyard, and the village enters each year the Best Kept Village Competition. The Best Kept Village plaque was proudly displayed in the old village, near to the village pump.

Waterfall 🦢

Contrary to expectation there is no waterfall in Waterfall, as many disappointed visitors have discovered. Its name derives from the fact that 'this water sinketh underground' – a not uncommon occurrence in summer in an area of limestone rock with swallow holes.

Waterfall is a picturesque Moorlands village of stone cottages and farms surrounded by the impressive scenery of its many hills and lows. Some of these lows or ancient burial grounds were excavated in the 19th century and revealed artefacts from the Bronze Age.

The oldest building in the village is, as in so many other villages, the parish church which dates from about 1100 and is certainly worth visiting with its fine Romanesque chancel arch and Jacobean screen. You may need to ask directions as the church is in a secluded, almost hidden, spot. The churchyard is unique in the county. It belongs to a lay rector, as it has done since the reign of James I.

Waterfall nestles around the village green on which are found the old pump, now disconnected, and the restored village stocks, no longer in use but an interesting feature to visitors. Also of interest is the old pinfold just down the lane where stray cattle were impounded until claimed by their owners on payment of a fine.

One of the many changes that have taken place in Waterfall is the closure of the village school. It was built in 1780 by the freeholders of Waterfall and land was given whose rent provided education for the children of the poor. A sad coincidence was that the school closed in its bicentennial year. However, it still serves Waterfall as a village hall and is well supported by many local organisations.

Winkhill, now noted only for its Trail Riding Centre was a busy industrial settlement in the 18th century, boasting mills producing leather, paper, flax, paint, dyes and corn. All of these were powered by water from the river Hamps. John Wesley preached at Winkhill and the old Methodist chapel, now a farm building was built in 1789. It was vacated 80 years ago because it was thought to be falling down!

Following the course of the river Hamps from Winkhill we reach Waterhouses now the largest village in the immediate area. Its position astride the river Hamps led to its growth in the days of turnpike roads. The railway came later, not only the North Staffordshire Railway but also the much shorter lived, though far more attractive, Leek and Manifold Valley Light Railway which opened in 1904 and closed 30 years later after proving uneconomic. The Manifold valley provides the visitor with beautiful scenery, abundant wildlife and wild flowers. An old disused quarry is now designated as an area of outstanding scientific and geological interest. The slopes of the valley that rise towards Calton are National Trust woods.

The oldest of these villages is Cauldon, which was mentioned in the Domesday Book. It has its own parish church whose present building is 18th century. Its modern altar is of local stone as this has been a quarrying village for over 200 years. The advent of the railway at the beginning of this century resulted in the building of houses and the immigration to the area of Welsh workers. The latest industry to arrive in the village was the cement works built 30 years ago but still one of the most modern plants in Europe. A far greater attraction in the village is the local inn noted for its amazing collection of curios and antiques and its real ale! A recently revived custom was the dressing of the village fountain in the manner of the Derbyshire well dressings.

Weston 🦐

Weston was an English forest clearing on the western boundary of the Chartley estate. Its original settlement was fertile, well drained land with a good water supply well above the flood plain of the river Trent. The modern estate roads of Outwoods Close and Wellyards Close are on this land. One of its great fields, is still recognisable – 'The Wadden', where woad was grown.

Weston is an ancient parish, formerly of greater area than it is today. Except for a small area owned by the Spencer family and the church lands of St Thomas' priory, Baswich and its lay successors it was part of the great Ferrers estate of Chartley until its sale in 1904. The Shirleys, Earls Ferrers, are remembered in Ferrers Road and the hamlet of Shirley-wich, the Spencers in Spencer Close and the priory of Saint Thomas in 'Abbeylands' (sic!) a Jacobean style house of 1858 by G G Scott.

The parish church of St Andrew was much restored by Scott in the 1860s and by Butterfield in the 1870s, when Norman work was found. The tower of the early 13th century is one of the finest Early English examples in the county. It only holds two bells, 'Ave Maria' of 1402 and 'Ann Shaw' of 1962. 'Katerena' of 1500 lies cracked upon the floor. There is a silver communion paten of the 15th century. The parish registers date from 1581.

Some old buildings remain. The present thatched manor house dates

172

from the 16th century in origin, and has been a farm building. It was in use from the mid 19th century as the National School and School Keeper's cottage; then as a Wesleyan Methodist meeting house until the present Methodist church was built at the turn of this century.

The old vicarage, opposite the church, dates from the 16th century and was the first of four vicarages all in a row on the 'New' Stafford Road.

A typical 1870 school building is now converted into a house. In Old Road is The Wellyards with its Victorian boat chandler's shop front, but with a 16th century cottage behind. It was the home of Ann Shaw, a village benefactress. Adjacent is the Bull Ring and The Cedars of 17th century origin as are cottages on The Green, Green Road and Stafford Road. These were the homes and workplaces of the village tradespeople.

All that are left of the buildings of Brindley's Trent and Mersey canal of 1777, are a hump bridge in Boat Lane, Weston lock and the canal itself. The wharves and warehouses for the saltworks at Shirleywich and at Saltworks Lane, the glueworks and the stone-mason's yard are all gone. The site of the Weston saltworks is now a light industrial estate.

Near the New Stafford Road crossing of the canal were the Nags Head, whose stables remain, the Boat Inn, which is now a house and the Saracen's Head still an inn. This latter name commemorates the grant of the crest of a 'Saracen's Head' to Lord Ferrers for his services to Richard Lionheart during the Third Crusade. The present inn sign is worth a closer look! The face of the crusader is that of the present landlord.

The village green belonged to the manor and was given to the Parish Council by the present Earl Ferrers, a Government Whip in the House of Lords. Since it was acquired, the Parish Council has added land enough to provide a football pitch for Weston's football club. It has been drained, levelled and planted with a variety of trees.

Weston is proud to be one of Staffordshire's Best Kept Villages. It entered the competition when it first started in 1956 and has won it many times since.

Wetley Rocks 🌿

The village has altered in many ways, but the main street still contains many of the original cottages built of stone obtained from a local quarry, which was part of the outcrop of rock dominating the area. The villagers were allowed to take away sandstone, without charge, to build their homes.

It is not surprising, therefore, that the latter part of the village name is derived from this same stone and huge outcrop of millstone grit, rising to a height of about 100 feet. The poor nature of the land is reflected in the word Wet Ley (meadows).

The two largest and most prestigious buildings in the area were Wetley Abbey, in its time the home of a well known painter, G H Mason and now a private nursing home and Westwood Manor, occupied by Colonel Thomas Powys who served under the Duke of Wellington. The Colonel in his will left the interest from the sum of £1000 to be distributed to the poor of the villages of Cheddleton and Wetley Rocks. After various owners the Manor came into the possession of Enoch Haughton and was given by him to Stoke-on-Trent Education Authority, to be used as a special school for children, in memory of his wife and it is still used for this purpose.

The spiritual welfare of the inhabitants was catered for by St John the Baptist church which was built in 1834 with stone from the local quarry and consecrated by the Right Reverend Henry Ryder, the then Bishop of Lichfield and Coventry. Following shortly after the erection of the church, the existing Wetley Rocks school was added in 1843 and so ended the Dame school in The Bunting.

The Methodist chapel, the first of which was in the main street of the village (now known as Chapel House) was built at a cost of £200 and later the existing chapel was erected to accommodate the larger congregation.

Although the village could not boast a doctor of its own, all the locals had great faith in Biddy Bailey, a local character who supplied pills and potions made with herbs.

Legend has it that when Bonnie Prince Charlie retreated northwards, some of his soldiers while resting on land at the top of the rocks, carved his initials on a stone in the garden of a local house and this stone can still be seen today.

A local custom in former years was the 'beating of the bounds', taking place once a year, which was the walking of the boundaries between the two villages of Wetley Rocks and Consall. The parish boundary passed through the public bar of the Plough Inn, and locals in carrying out this annual event, were known to risk life and limb by scaling and walking over the roof of the hostelry.

174

One of the unchanging attractive features of the area is the magnificent scenic backdrop afforded by the distant hills of the Peak District. However, Wetley Rocks today has seen little development, apart from the addition of a small number of modern homes, the owners of which make up a typical cross section of today's modern technological age.

One cannot mention the name of Wetley Rocks without thinking of the hamlet of Consall. Consall has always been closely linked with the village, joining in its community life. It has few amenities of its own other than a single public house in the well known Consall Forge, now being developed as a public recreation area, but previously known as 'the hidden valley'. Access on foot is down a stairway of over 200 steps and known as 'the devil's staircase'.

Whiston

Whiston is a village of approximately 400 inhabitants nestling on a hillside, approached by the notorious Whiston bank between Cheadle and Ashbourne. It is of a scattered nature beginning at the Leys and meandering on the side of the A52 to Brook Hollow. Dominating the village is a dark stone house known as Whiston Hall, unfortunately not inhabited today, but used by the golf club.

Although Whiston is very small in terms of inhabitants, it boasts a golf course, a public house, garage with full facilities, general store and post office, this being a listed building with the unique feature of an 8-sided dovecote built into the roof. The village also has a recreation ground, a village garden, the ground being purchased, designed and created by local subscriptions and labour to commemorate the Queen's Silver Jubilee 1977. There is a primary school, chapel and church, the latter being built in the 1920s from donated stone and local labour. The latest addition to the village is a magnificent village hall built after 18 years fund raising.

In the late 19th century Whiston saw copper smelting, copper being brought from Ecton by rail and smelted on what is now known as the works yard. The only visual sign of the old workings is the house once known as 'the shop' which was in fact the offices of the old smelting works. The other outstanding feature is Stable House, Black Lane. This is built of blocks of slag which contain a certain percentage of copper,

Whiston village

which was the residue of the ore smelting and formed into blocks. There are only one or two other places in the country where these blocks have been used.

Like many villages Whiston is not without its ghosts. Although now demolished, the second largest house in the village was a Georgian country house known as Whiston Eaves which for many years was reputed to be haunted, and perhaps this was one of the reasons that the house fell into a state of disrepair. The house was connected with the murder of Thomas Smith junior, son of the Lord of the Manor of Whiston Eaves, his murderer being the last person to be hung publicly outside Stafford gaol on the 7th August 1866.

The old village was mainly dependent on agriculture, with a percentage of the male population later being employed at the copper works of Froghall and Oakamoor. In 1959 British Industrial Sand began quarrying the area, this also provided employment for villagers and local people.

Whitmore 🐚

Anyone driving at speed along the A53 Newcastle to Market Drayton road, would see little of Whitmore village except the Mainwaring Arms public house and a few white-washed cottages. Not that the village is a large one, but those who walk in it never fail to be delighted by it.

The original village dwellings follow the line of the old road from Newcastle, through Butterton and Aston, over the A53 and up the hill behind the former rectory to Whitmore Heath and Baldwin's Gate. Indeed, the modern extended village reaches as far as the railway line, encompassing Whitmore Heath, Coneygreave and Appleton Drive.

Many of the villagers are still employed in agriculture, others travel to town to work. A craft gallery and tea room have contributed to the attraction for the visitor.

Only yards from the busy main road, opposite the Mainwaring Arms, the church of St Mary and All Saints nestles among the trees. Parts of the church building date from the 12th century and the pretty west face shows the 17th century black and white timbered bell tower to advantage. The black and white porch beneath is Victorian. Inside, the church is of simple layout and decoration, apart from the screen behind the altar which is ornately patterned in tile and mosaic, in blues and golds, dating from 1880 when the church was restored by a member of the Minton-Hollins family.

From the churchyard, at the end of a long avenue of lime trees, Whitmore Hall can be seen amid rhododendrons and rolling parkland. This imposing brick and stone fronted building, and the surrounding estate are owned by the Cavanagh-Mainwaring family and have been passed by direct line, sometimes through an heiress, from generation to generation since Norman times, which must be something of a record.

Admiral Mainwaring, who occupied the Hall from 1837 till he died in 1862, saw the completion of the new main road in 1846 and insisted that it be cut low enough, as it went through his parkland, that users might not be seen from the Hall and its grounds. Fortunately for the present occupants few double-decked buses use the road! He was responsible for building the Mainwaring Arms and the Sheet Anchor, the latter to serve travellers who used Whitmore station.

There is a decided feeling of the past and present meeting in the village, and it is not difficult to imagine Whitmore in bygone ages. Despite the noise from the main road, and even from the motorway sometimes, depending on the wind direction, there is tranquillity.

Whittington 🌿

Whittington, originally Hwitantone (Wita's town), is mentioned in the history books as far back as the year 1200. The village is sitauated 3 miles south-east of Lichfield and approximately 3 miles west of Tamworth. In the year 1817, records show that 602 people resided in Whittington but now it boasts a population of over 3000.

St Giles, the local church, was constructed in the 13th century from sandstone quarried from nearby Hopwas Wood. The Jacobean pulpit was originally made for Lichfield cathedral where it remained for 118 years. In 1789 it was transferred to the neighbouring church of St Peter's at Elford. During a restoration period at St Peter's the pulpit was discarded in old stables on land belonging to Miss Mary Dyott's mother's family. Here it lay in oblivion for 74 years until Miss Dyott's grandfather offered it to St Giles. To make the pulpit fit into the church it had to be sunk into the floor.

Freeford Manor, home of the Dyott family, is believed to have been used as a leper hospital – perhaps that is why the church once named for St Matthew became St Giles, St Giles being the patron saint of beggars and lepers.

Whittington heath opposite Freeford Manor was once 600 acres of open land. Barley and turnips were the main vegetables grown on this land, the soil being the most suitable for growing these crops in the country. The Marquis of Anglesey owned Whittington heath and 338 acres were later used as Lichfield racecourse, where racing continued until 1890. Frequent visitors to Lichfield races were Sir Robert Peel, of the Metropolitan Police fame, and King Edward VII, the latter staying at Whittington Old Hall. The whole of Whittington heath was purchased from the Marquis of Anglesey in 1881 by the War Department and the grandstand belonging to the racecourse (now Whittington Barracks Golf Clubhouse) became a soldiers' barracks and was used as such until 1955.

The original Old Hall was reputed to have been constructed in the 1500s and the building which stands today was built in 1891. Only the garden gateway and the two gate piers dated 1673 are part of the original building. Originally the Old Hall was the home of the Babingtons who became involved with the downfall of Mary Queen of Scots. It is now divided into two and privately owned.

The newly erected church hall was named after Thomas Spencer (of Marks and Spencer) who once lived in Darnford Lane and is buried in the churchyard.

In 1741 a free school was endowed by Sarah Neale, a wealthy property owner and in 1864 a new school building was erected in Main Street with the help of a legacy of £200 made by Reverend Richard Levett in 1800. Several years ago parents undertook the renovation of the school building and it has since been used as a youth club and pre-school play centre.

In 1926 a newly qualified nurse came to the village and here she spent the rest of her full-time working days nursing and delivering babies. In 1964 Her Majesty the Queen was graciously pleased to award Nurse Darby the MBE for her work in the community. This still very popular lady was into the third generation of baby delivering when she went into semi-retirement to nurse old folk!

St Giles' Hospice, first thought about in 1979, was officially opened by

HRH the Princess Alexandra on the 27th September 1983, although the first patient was admitted in April 1983.

Wigginton 🦚

The small pleasant village of Wigginton is about 1½ miles north east of Tamworth. It is mentioned in the Domesday Book as being 'held by the King'. There are ancient earthworks in and around the village and many coins and ancient human bones have been dug up, especially in an area called 'Low Flat' or 'Moneylands'.

It has always been an agricultural area and is so today, but now only a few of the inhabitants are agricultural workers. Most are business people who commute to the towns, or professional people.

In 1238 the manor of Wigginton was granted to Henry de Hastings, a baron who joined Simon de Montfort against King Henry III and consequently lost all his possessions to Sir Philip Marmion. In later years the Lordship went to the de Comberford family, who were also dispossessed by choosing the wrong side in the Civil War. No-one seems to know where the manor house was sited, but there is in existence an imposing farmhouse called Manor House Farm. There is no longer a Lord of the Manor.

A Saxon highway used to run through Wigginton from Tamworth, thought to have been a salt track. There are still signs of the old track, and a road called Salters Lane on the Tamworth side. The roads in the 17th century were very poor, being impassable for many months of the year.

In 1274 Sir Philip Marmion caused to be built the hospital of St James for the Premonstratensian Order near the Ashby Road. Later a chapel was built to serve the hospital. The hospital no longer exists, but the chapel which was in disuse for many years, was found to have been used for a time as a barn, then as a cottage. It was restored in 1914 since when it has been used for special services, and is now known as 'the Spital chapel'.

The parish church of St Leonard was built of red brick in 1779, 'so that the parishioners could worship in comfort, and not have to travel in bad weather' (presumably to Tamworth). In 1830 the church was enlarged, the new part being built of stone, making 270 sittings of which 142 were free.

In 1849 the Wigginton National school was built by subscription at a cost of £330, which served until the 1960s when a new school was built. The National school was then turned into the village hall many of the villagers helping to raise the money towards the project.

A very famous character from the 17th Century was Mary Vaughan who was renowned because she took so little sustenance. She lived in Wigginton, and was supposed 'never to have eaten more food in a day than a piece of bread and butter the size of a half crown, or if meat, not above the size of a pigeon's egg, nor if drink more than a spoonful of milk or water. Yet she was a healthy maiden, of fresh complexion and piously disposed'.

The New Crown is now a dwelling house, and the only Public House is The Old Crown. Years ago there was a Post Office, first in a farmhouse, then in a cottage, but alas, that and the village shop are no more.

Wombourne 🌿

Wombourne is a large overgrown village in the south-west corner of the county, close to the bounds of both Shropshire and Worcestershire. The A449 road goes through on the east side and the Staffordshire and Worcestershire canal on the west. Through the middle flows little Wom Brook on its way to the rivers Stour and Severn. 'Wombourne' is how most inhabitants spell it, although a few prefer 'Wombourn'.

The ancient parish church of St Benedict Biscop was the only one in England so dedicated. Benedict was a 7th century Northumbrian bishop who founded monasteries at Jarrow and Monkwearmouth, and is the patron saint of glassmakers. Benedict's teaching and his precious library were the basis of the future works of Bede, the great scholar, theologian and historian (AD 673–735). Therefore it made good sense when, nearly 13 centuries later, a daughter church was built to serve the needs of the growing parish of Wombourne, that the people should choose him as its saint. Now in the 1980s the two Anglican churches share the care of the parish with St Bernadette's Roman Catholic church, a United Reformed church and a Methodist church.

The oldest dwelling in the village is The Wodehouse (pronounced Woodhouse), an attractive mansion in wide grounds above the brook on the eastern edge of the parish. About 1180 William le Coq was granted a clearing in the forest and later built his 'house in the wood'. His descendants, the Woodhouse family, lived on this site until the beginning of the 18th century, after which it passed to the Helliers, Shaw Helliers and in 1981 to Mr John Phillips. The core of the present building is a late medieval timber-framed house, and all around it are the additions and alterations from the late 16th to the 19th centuries, the whole being a fascinating home. The owners share the house and grounds with the villagers for fetes and other fund raising activities.

The lower section of the 'Staffs and Worcester' through Wombourne and beyond, is reckoned to be one of the loveliest lengths of canal in England. James Brindley's masterpiece (opened 1772) is a contour canal with the natural curves of the river valleys it follows. It was a vital link in his scheme for connecting the Trent and Mersey canal with the river Severn. Two centuries on Brindley's canal is an amenity, a place for leisure and pleasure. People come to marvel at the Bratch locks, where the land drops sharply for 30 feet, and admire their complicated but efficient construction.

Time has healed the landscape wounds caused by the coming of the railway and the deserted trackway is now a most pleasant path, officially called the Kingswinford Branch Railway Walk. The station building is the information centre for Nature Trails and various other local walks. Only the elderly villagers can hear in their memory the big steam engine's whistle as the driver took it through the cutting in the woods.

In 1750 Wombourne was purely agricultural (a mere handful of men worked in a nearby iron forge), by 1800 there was horticulture as well. By 1850 there was sand mining and a spell of the hand-made nail trade, but until the middle of the next century there was no great leap in the population. The national boundary upheaval in the 1970s broke Wombourne's link with its Saxon heritage when the old Seisdon Hundred lost its identity in the South Staffs District build-up. In the 1980s Wombourne has acquired many new amenities, but it still thinks and behaves like a village in the real caring sense of the word.

Woodseaves 🌿

Woodseaves is a small village situated on the A519 between Eccleshall and Newport.

Woodseaves is in the parish of High Offley and for many years the centre of worship for Anglicans was the church of St Mary the Virgin, High Offley. Villagers could also attend the church of St Lawrence at Gnosall. However, in the 1830s the villagers petitioned for a new church to be built and the Earl of Lichfield gave a piece of land in Knightley for the purpose. The church was opened for worship in 1844. In the early 1970s, Knightley too was taken into the parish of High Offley.

The Methodist chapel was built in the last quarter of the 19th century on the crossroads of the High Offley and Eccleshall roads, a prominent site now in the centre of the village.

The school at Knightley was originally a National school, opened in 1844. The land was given by the Earl of Lichfield and, after a new school opened in Woodseaves in 1969, the building was used as the estate office for the Lichfield estate until it was sold in 1979. It is now a private house of character.

During the early 1950s rapid development took place in the village with council houses being built, followed by bungalows and two private estates.

Although the village is no longer self-sufficent, it still has a shop, post office, garage and school, as well as three local pubs.

Wootton 🌿

The impressive 1200 foot limestone summit of the Weaver Hill with its Bronze Age barrow stands wild and majestic overshadowing the tiny village of Wootton.

Wootton or 'Wood-town' is built of the sandstone that forms a sort of skirt round the lower half of the Weaver and, where the limestone and the sandstone rocks meet, springs come to the surface. Bidner Spring is still in use and serves about six households in the village and at one time was the water supply for Wootton Hall. Wootton has three wells: Nook

Well, Delbert Lane and Hall Lane. Mains water only arrived in Wootton in 1962 and, before that, all drinking water was carried in buckets and churns from the Nook Well which was never known to dry up. Water for other purposes was obtained from the rain water troughs that every householder had. A spring runs right through the village and milk from the farms used to be cooled by standing the churns in it.

Wootton Hall was situated below the village in a wooded valley with a stream but is now demolished. In the 18th century it was owned by the Bromley Davenports of Capesthorne Hall in Cheshire. The Wootton Hall and Ellastone estates owned by General Sir W Bromley Davenport were auctioned at the Green Man at Ashbourne on 16th May 1929: practically the whole of the two villages extending to an area of about 2,524 acres.

In 1766 Mr Davenport lent Wootton Hall to the French writer, Jean-Jacques Rousseau. Accompanied by his housekeeper, Mlle Thérèse Le Vasseur, he was to stay at Wootton Hall for 14 months. The bleak weather did not really suit him and he was somewhat haunted by the belief that he was the victim of a conspiracy and suffered great bouts of depression. For example, he thought that attempts were being made to poison him by putting cinders in his soup.

Old village place names are now only used by those who have lived or been connected with Wootton for many generations. Old Dumble Lane which was used to carry stone from the quarries on the Weaver and Giggity Lane (Gig Acre) nearby Shawcroft Farm. A field at the base of the Weaver they refer to as Target Field because it was used by the army in the First World War for target practice and was again used by the Home Guard in the Second World War.

The Domesday Book refers to the land at Wootton as 'waste': common or open land. Most of the 1,549 acres at Wootton is now owned and administered by the Silcock estate although some land on the west side is owned by the Bamford family.

The Silcock estate have reduced the number of farms to two economical units and sold off surplus houses and barns for conversion to dwellings, so few of the population of 100 are now involved in agriculture. Erstwhile farms, barns and buildings are used for different pursuits; goat herds for milk, yoghurt and angora wool; specialist breeds of sheep; free range chickens for eggs; fruit and Christmas tree growing; a joinery; and a sculpture and art studio of great renown run by Simon and Lee

Manby. But many of the stone cottages and farmhouses set in their large plots of land and separated from their neighbours by dry stone walls have been lovingly restored by people who have chosen to make their homes in this picturesque village and travel out of it to work.

The North entrance of Wootton Hall

Wrinehill

The village of Wrinehill once boasted its own 'Dr' Johnson. Samuel Johnson was born on 13th October 1838. He hoped to become a doctor but owing to deaths in the family he returned home to Wrinehill and became a draper and general merchant. Later he fulfilled his ambition to become an apothecary.

Samuel Johnson acquired what had previously been the Red Lion public house, built some 300 years earlier, and it soon became known as the Medicine House. Here he made up the patent medicine called 'The Staffordshire Cure All'. This was packed into little pottery jars which had the picture of the Summer House on the front. Might *you* own a very old bottle labelled 'Johnsons Oils'? A number of people in Wrinehill and Betley do.

If you pass through Wrinehill look out for the Summer House which has stood high above the surrounding countryside since 1700, when it belonged to the Egertons of Wrinehill – as did the Hall and the Red Lion. Pause at the present Wrinehill post office. The part which is the house, built in 1750, is referred to in the deeds as The Manor House. Who kept a shop here? Our apothecary friend Samuel Johnson. Along with his shop at the Summer House he gained a reputation as one who stocked everything. The post office was later opened by his son in 1909 and run for many years by his grandson into the late 1960s.

What of the old Medicine House? When local sewers were laid in the roadway in 1963 the house began to crack. Later the roof was in need of repair. So, in February 1969 the Medicine House was sold. To begin with its whereabouts were a mystery but today it can be seen from the railway as the Crewe/Manchester train passes through Goostrey.

Yoxall ᘓᕊᕀ

The name Yoxall has been variously interpreted, but the Saxon origin of 'Yox' from 'yoke of oxen' and 'all' from 'halgh' meaning a 'hidden place', seems appropriate as the village is indeed tucked into a hollow on the banks of the river Swarbourn.

Many old houses and cottages remain in the village, but with changing needs few serve their original purpose. The 17th century grange, with its Dutch gables, was once the rectory (with a priest hole). The Hollies, a three storey Georgian property housed a tape mill. Reeve End Cottage, (dated as pre-1350), is the only known aisled hall remaining in Staffordshire. Hairdresser and newsagent shops now occupy the site where once the village smithy stood; a traffic island has replaced the farmers' weighbridge; Tom Paget's shop in Hadley Street was removed in its entirety and re-assembled as a typical 'Victorian village store' in the Staffordshire County Museum at Shugborough; Birmingham House, now an antiques shop, is an early 17th century timber-framed building which was once the home of George Walton, grandfather of Izaac Walton. Later this double-fronted building was occupied by a saddler, whose wares were exhibited in the one window whilst the taxidermist's display in the other must have struck terror into the hearts of local wildlife.

186

Having been bypassed by both the canal and railway systems of the Industrial Revolution, their accompanying employment and affluence were lost to Yoxall, but the agricultural community survived, with farms, trades and crafts being handed down from father to son. The self-contained character of the village was retained. It is not surprising therefore, that many local families, such as the Lesters, Johnsons, Matthews, Heathcots and others can trace their ancestry back hundreds of years. This stability of population was probably contributed to by the known long service of certain rectors and schoolmasters, as well as by the three generations of Armsons, who as doctors, administered to the community. One of the Armson doctors, it is said, operated the following system of remunerations: 'For the rich he prescribed and took pay, For the poor his advice gave away'.

Despite the absence of a ghost, Yoxall has its own phenomenon; of less substance than a ghost, imperceptible to the human eye but sensed by many a shying horse at the spot where the skeleton of a boy, run through with a spear, was discovered. Research has shown that the ill-treated blacksmiths' apprentice committed suicide whilst his employer was at church. It could be that the youth's affinity with horses during his lifetime evoked the 'presence' to linger over his grave in the unconsecrated ground.

Yoxall today is a busy community with its amalgam of ancient and modern and many residents are obliged to commute daily to Burton-on-Trent, Lichfield or Birmingham owing to the dearth of local employment. Numerous clubs and societies flourish, providing pleasure and involvement for all ages.

The beautiful countryside around with its many lanes, half-closed with Queen Anne's Lace in springtime, affords much pleasure to hikers, cyclists and riders, whilst a glimpse of the heron fishing the Swarbourn or the rare sighting of a Goldcrest, or the Little Owl at dusk is pure joy to the local ornithologist.

Colton village

Index

189

191